Going to the Root

GOING TO THE
ROOT

*Nine Proposals for
Radical Church Renewal*

Christian Smith

HERALD PRESS
Scottdale, Pennsylvania
Waterloo, Ontario

Library of Congress Cataloging-in-Publication Data
Smith, Christian (Christian Stephen), 1960-
   Going to the root : nine proposals for radical church renewal /
Christian Smith.
    p. cm.
  Includes bibliographical references.
  ISBN 0-8361-3584-9
  1. Church renewal. I. Title.
BV600.2.S574 1992
262'.001'7—dc20
                                       92-3591
                                          CIP

The paper used in this publication is recycled and meets the minimum
requirements of American National Standard for Information Sci-
ences—Permanence of Paper for Printed Library Materials, ANSI
Z39.48-1984.

Grateful acknowledgment is made to Harper Collins publishers for
permission to quote, on p. 109, from C. S. Lewis, *The Silver Chair* (New
York, Macmillan Child Group, 1988).

00 99 98 97 96 95 94 93 92 10 9 8 7 6 5 4 3 2 1

For Jack & Jeanine Skeen
who opened the door
and
for Jack Miller
who pushed me through it

Contents

Author's Preface

IT IS interesting to me that Herald Press, a Mennonite publisher, chose to publish *Going to the Root*. Although I am not a Mennonite, many of the ideas I present in this book stem from earlier encounters with the Anabaptist values Mennonites affirm.

When I was a teenager, my family moved to Harleysville, Pennsylvania, an area rich in Mennonite culture. Although many ethnic groups are now included in the Mennonite church, back then in that area Swiss-German Mennonites predominated. It seemed all our new neighbors were named Bergey, Ruth, Alderfer, Stoltzfus, and Yoder.

I was raised a Presbyterian and continued to commute some distance to a Presbyterian church. But my parents' search for a church closer to home led them to explore a number of local Mennonite and Brethren churches. We were thus exposed to Anabaptist thought, and spent many hours discussing the Anabaptist call to discipleship, service, pacifism, community, simplicity, and so on.

Something in Anabaptism sparked my imagination. I

read a variety of Anabaptist-oriented authors, including John Howard Yoder, Donald Kraybill, Ronald Sider, Walter Klaassen, J. C. Wenger, Dave and Neta Jackson, and Jim Wallis. I had reservations—yet it seemed I had stumbled onto a promising vision of Christianity.

This exploration of Anabaptism continued in college. Through a class field trip, I discovered Reba Place Fellowship, a Mennonite intentional Christian community in Evanston, Illinois. Soon I was attending Reba Place regularly.

I continued reading the history and theology of Anabaptism. I even remember telling a Mennonite college friend of mine, shortly before dropping out of the evangelical college I attended, that he was crazy for coming to that school. Why hadn't he instead attended one in his own tradition, since Anabaptism had a far better understanding of Christianity than evangelicalism did?

My encounter with Anabaptism shaped my thinking about Christianity and the church, although I never actually fully "converted" and became a Mennonite. Anabaptism has remained influential in my reflections in the years since.

There is a second reason why the Herald Press decision to publish this book interests me. Publishing companies choose works they think their constituents want and need. Do Anabaptists, I wonder, want and need to hear the message of this book? If so, if in my eclectic reformulation of Anabaptist and other thought I have perhaps arrived at something helpful to Anabaptists, I am gratified. Perhaps through this book I can, in a small way, repay the Anabaptist tradition for all I have taken from it.

In the end, however, what I might have to offer Anabaptist churches is nothing more than a call to be their true selves. For the basic message here is simply a restated version of the original insight of Anabaptism. And that is that the standard, taken-for-granted forms of Christian church

—today no less than in the sixteenth century—are inadequate, cumbersome, and unbiblical. Thus nothing less than radical change will put us where we ought to be.

Let me not forget to thank Robert and Julie Banks, Stan Gaede, Mark Lamport, Lois Barrett, and Hilary Noble for critical responses to all or part of this manuscript.

— *Christian Smith*
Salem, Massachusetts

INTRODUCTION

Church Renewal
That Goes to the Root

MANY CHRISTIANS know that the church today needs serious renewal. The many articles, books, sermons, and seminars on church renewal in recent years verify the widespread realization among Christians that the church is not all that it could or should be. Inspired by a desire to serve God more faithfully, Christians of many traditions are exploring ways to renew the church.

Yet this common agreement about the *need* for renewal has not translated into common *strategies* for renewal. Indeed, the list of strategies for church renewal is long. Some advocate miraculous signs and wonders as the key to renewal. Others think the answer is a return to traditional liturgy. One school of thought argues for intense evangelistic outreach. Another experiments with the formation of small groups. Yet another calls for a new focus on prayer.

How do we make sense of these myriad renewal strategies? Is one as good as another? Clearly each idea may contain some insight, some understanding of the church's problems. Each deserves consideration.

Yet if we are serious about church renewal, we will need to go farther and deeper than most of these proposed strategies. To accomplish the required renewal, we'll have to do more than scratch the surface, as many of these strategies seem to me to do. Most churches today don't need mere revival or rejuvenation—they need serious overhaul. It's not just a matter of slapping on a new coat of paint, but of structural renovation. Christians need to go to the root.

The problem with many approaches to church renewal is not that they come up with the wrong answer—but that they don't ask the right question. Most begin by asking "What strategy or program will work best to revitalize this church?" Wrong question. We need to dig deeper.

The right question is often not how to revitalize the churches we have. The right question is "Do we even have the correct vision for what our church ought to be in the first place?" In other words, the first and most important issue, when it comes to thinking about church renewal, ought not to be *pragmatic* ("How can we do it?") but *normative* ("What really ought we to do?").

Jim Wallis has observed, "Repairs in the road are useless if the road is heading in the wrong direction." This book is about trying to head church renewal in the right direction. It is about getting a clearer vision, a better idea of what churches should look like, so that our efforts at renewal take us where we really ought to go.

Before we plunge into the work of renewing the churches we have today, we need to step back for a moment and dream. We must mentally put aside our immediate church situations and visualize what the Christian church *ought* to be, what it *should* look like.

Imagine a church brimming with life. Picture a church where people really know and love each other in concrete ways. Imagine a congregation where fellowship, encouragement, support, prayer, and accountability are not just words—but a natural part of everyday relationships. Envision a church that feels like a community or an extended family, that is not so much something that people go to, but something people together *are*. Picture a congregation in which ordinary people take responsibility for what needs to be done, where each member participates and shares gifts for the good of the whole church.

Consider a body of believers for whom the Christian faith is not just a belief system, but an authentic life experience. Imagine a church more interested in Christian growth and transformation than its own routine maintenance and stability. Envision a church where ordinary believers are empowered to minister the love of God in a natural way in jobs, schools, and neighborhoods.

Imagine a body of Christians whose lives are shaped as much by the kingdom of God as by surrounding culture—so people actually have reason to sit up, take notice, and ask, "What makes those Christians live so differently?"

Is this not what the Christian church should look like? Is this not what we are called to? If so, it is clear that many churches need more than a mere rejuvenation. They need a radical church renewal that goes to the root.

Church renewal requires things to change. This seems obvious. Yet many people want church renewal that doesn't require fundamental personal or congregational change. They want things basically the same, only better. That's because change is difficult. But real renewal without real change can't take place.

Radical church renewal requires basic changes both in our *consciousness* and our *structures*. A change in consciousness means an overturning of our common values, thoughts, and expectations. Unfortunately, to paraphrase an old adage, you can take some people out of an old, stale church, but you can't take the old, stale church out of some people. In other words, to be successful, renewal demands that we change how we *think* about church as well as how we practice church.

Radical church renewal also means changing church structures. Renewal demands that we alter—and sometimes eliminate—many institutional practices, rules, roles, and programs.

What big changes, specifically, does radical church renewal entail? What kind of overall vision will guide these changes? Where will this vision come from?

The vision proposed in this book does not have its origins in school classrooms. It has not been invented by denominational leaders or academic theologians. Rather, it grows out of the experience of a grass-roots, Christian movement.

All over the world—from Ontario to China, Brazil to Scotland, Uganda to Australia—Christians have been building a movement that is quietly transforming the church. This movement has received such names as "the people's church," "base ecclesial communities," "the house-church movement," "intentional Christian community," "the popular church."

Despite the variety of labels, at the core of the movement lies a dynamic vision of what the church can and should be. This vision weaves together the themes of community, participation, spiritual growth, celebration, service to the poor, discipleship, mutual accountability, and social transformation into a fresh experience of church.

It is exactly this dynamic vision that offers North American churches a promising direction for effective church renewal today. The vision can guide us to transform our churches into what we know they should be, yet hardly dare hope they can be.

What follows are nine concrete proposals, drawn from

this vision, that most North American churches serious about renewal can implement. Each proposal aims to transform a key element of church life—such as ministry, decision making, leadership, worship, evangelism, or spirituality.

These proposals are not perfect and require testing and ongoing refinement. They are not offered as universally binding demands, but as one alternative for churches interested in radical renewal. I hope that those ready for radical church renewal will find that implementing these nine proposals can allow God to transform their churches, and possibly their lives, from the bottom up.

Going to the Root

1

Build Intentional Christian Community

RADICAL CHURCH RENEWAL begins with a new vision of Christian relationships in the body of Christ. It begins with the conviction that the church should not be a place of casual acquaintanceships but of committed community. It affirms that the church should look and feel, not like a club or interest group, but a loving, extended family.

The model discussed below is most easily applied to smaller churches with the possibility of regular intimacy among all members. Thus it is important to note that community may take different shapes in different settings. Some large churches, for instance, remain a loose association of Christians at the level of the entire group. Yet if one looks closely, one might find within smaller groupings the characteristics of true community.

Whatever shape community takes in a specific situation, the Bible does teach clearly how Christians should live together. Christians are called to be at peace with each other (Mark 9:50). To wash each other's feet (John 13:14). To be members of each other (Rom. 12:5). To be devoted to each other (Rom. 12:10). To honor each other above themselves (Rom. 12:10). To live in harmony with each other (Rom. 12:16). Not to judge each other (Rom. 14:13). To build up each other (Rom. 14:19). To be like-minded toward each other (Rom. 15:5).

Christians are to admonish each other (Rom. 15:14). To greet each other with a holy kiss (Rom. 16:16; 1 Cor. 16:20; 2 Cor. 13:12; 1 Pet. 5:14). To wait for each other (1 Cor. 14:27). To care for each other (1 Cor. 12:25). To serve each other (Gal. 5:13). To bear with each other (Eph. 4:2; Col. 3:13). To speak truthfully to each other (Eph. 1.25) Col 3:9). To be kind and compassionate to each other (Eph. 4:32). To submit to each other (Eph. 5:21). To forgive each other (Col. 3:13). To comfort each other (1 Thess. 4:18).

Still the list goes on. Christians are to incite each other to love and good deeds (Heb. 10:24). To encourage each other (Heb. 10:25). Not to speak evil of each other (James 4:11). Not to complain against each other (James 5:9). To confess sins to each other (James 5:16). To pray for each other (James 5:16). To offer hospitality to each other (1 Pet. 4:9). To be humble toward each other (1 Pet. 5:5). To have fellowship with each other (1 John 1:7). To love each other (John 13:34-35; 15:12, 17; Rom. 13:8; 1 Thess. 3:12; 4:9; 1 Pet. 1:22; 1 John 3:11, 23; 4:7, 11-12; 2 John 5).

Think for a moment. What is necessary for people to live like this? People must truly know each other, share with each other who they really are. People must spend a great deal of time together, living so their daily lives interact closely. People living this way communicate regularly, in an atmosphere of commitment, trust, and acceptance. They need to be devoted to each other's growth and well-being.

Christian community happens when believers share daily life in pursuit of the kingdom of God. Community is a place where all members experiences fellowship and acceptance because they belong to a web of loving, committed relationships. Christian community means living a life of interdependence, support, service, communion, sharing, and solidarity with brothers and sisters in Christ. It involves celebrating our joys and triumphs as well as struggling to move through problems and conflicts toward unity and reconciliation.

Community means more than having good friends. It means being part of a body of people committed to extraordinary relationships rooted in a common identity and purpose in Christ. Community means more than having lots of meetings. It means jointly building a way of life, a group memory, and a common, anticipated future. Community also means more than getting cozy in exclusive, ingrown support groups. Community is lived in the world, openly and inclusively.

Christians can't fully live out the Bible's call without living in community. Thus living in Christian community is not an option a few fanatics might choose. God calls all believers into community.

Belonging to a church means more than having our names on a list and attending Sunday services. It means being members of an extended family or household (Gal. 6:10; Eph. 2:19; Heb. 3:6; 1 Pet. 4:17) whose ties are stronger than those of our natural families (Luke 8:20-21). All believers are called to *koinōnia*, to an experience of deep fellowship, sharing, and communion (Acts 2:42; 1 John 1:3,7; Philem. 6).

Believing in Christ does not simply make us new individuals who meet together weekly. It makes us a new race, a new nation. It turns us into the people of God, into citizens of a new kind of city (Titus 2:14; 1 Pet. 2:9-10; Phil. 3:20; Heb. 13:14). It is this collective identity, this experience of fellowship as the family and people of God, which

Christian community seeks to express.

Unfortunately, many churches believe these ideas in the abstract. But because their structures and practices obstruct the actual experience of Christian community, they encourage casual and sometimes even shallow relationships. Far too many Christians only see each other a few hours a week on Sunday mornings (and maybe Wednesday evenings).

During the week such Christians live their separate lives, like every other person in society, busy with commitments to a host of other people and organizations. "Fellowship" then becomes little more than a few Sunday morning handshakes, occasional chats over coffee and cookies, and a yearly church picnic. Church members may be inspired by a sermon on Christian love even though they don't even know the names of the people sitting in the pew next to them. Radical church renewal changes this. It builds Christian community.

A Closer Look at Christian Community

People often confuse living in community and living communally. Living in community does not require sharing living quarters and bank accounts (though that is possible). Sharing life in daily relationships matters more than exactly who owns what and who lives with whom. And sometimes communal living creates more difficulties than benefits.

Nonetheless, while community need not equal communal living, it does require sharing life. And this often requires that Christians live near each other and share many of the routines of daily life.

In the church community I belong to, most of us live in the same town. Many members have intentionally bought houses and rented apartments near each other. In my neighborhood cluster, five church families own or rent houses on one street corner.

This makes it possible and natural to interact daily. We don't have to schedule meetings and drive our cars to see each other. We run into each other on our front porches. Living next to each other makes it easy and natural to take care of each other's children, to eat dinner together spontaneously, to play badminton after work, to share the newspaper. It also makes it more likely that we know when one of us is going through a difficult time and needs help, prayer, or support.

Living in community can involve sharing possessions. For example, some in our church cooperatively own multifamily houses. Indeed, my wife and I were able to first buy into a cooperatively owned house when another church family gave us half the down payment money. More recently, four families in our neighborhood cluster bought a lawn mower together. Others in our church community have purchased cars, boats, and tools together. By sharing money and possessions in such ways, we both concretely express our love for each other and are good stewards of the resources God has entrusted to us.

In our church, living in community also means helping each other work on our houses. Recently, someone needed a room in her house painted before renting it to a boarder. She announced this in church. The next Saturday morning a handful of us showed up with tools and finished the job in a few hours. Afterward, we ate lunch together and discussed issues of leadership and decision making in the church. In a similar way, people in our church have freely helped each other remodel kitchens, build porches, tear down plaster, and wallpaper rooms.

Christian community can also be expressed by turning the drudgery of moving to a new house into a party. When anyone in our church has to move, we all arrive early for doughnuts and coffee. Then, with much laughter and jest, we form a human chain and pass all the boxes and furniture down the stairs, out the door, and onto the truck.

A few stay behind to clean up the old place, but most form another chain at the new house. When all the boxes and furniture have been passed by the chain into the house, the host plugs in the stereo and breaks out the pizza, soda, and ice cream.

In this way, my wife and I recently had the contents of our entire house moved *in less than two hours*. Not only does this make life easier for the people moving, but everyone has a great time. Our unity and love are expressed through the cooperation and service involved in moving.

Community is also built and enjoyed through celebrations. Our community uses almost any excuse to get together to eat, drink, dance, and generally enjoy each other. We have as many wedding showers, housewarming parties, baby showers, graduation parties, birthday parties, and holiday celebrations as possible. Our New Year's Eve party is especially important. We collect slides taken during the year for a slide show to together remember our community's events of the last twelve months.

Community is also woven together through a variety of other group rituals and habits. For example, every year on Easter morning, our church wakes up early. We walk to a park overlooking the ocean and sings Easter hymns as the sun rises. Afterward, we walk to a nearby house and enjoy a pancake breakfast.

During the summer, one group plays basketball every Sunday afternoon, while another barbecues together every Monday night. I play badminton with my next-door neighbor three times a week. Some in our community prepare and serve a meal together for the homeless at a local soup kitchen every month. Others get together regularly to support and care for women suffering after abortions.

When someone in our church delivers a baby or is sick, we bring them hot meals until they are on their feet again. In September, we all pack up and spend a weekend retreat at a camp in the New Hampshire woods. There, after a lazy, scattered summer, we focus our thoughts and hearts on entering a new season together. Throughout the year we watch and discuss movies together, go food shopping together, commute to work together, play cards together, and spend weekend vacations together.

Not everyone enjoys this much togetherness, it must be granted. Christians who require significant space and time alone to maintain contact with their souls should not be made to think this is invalid. But in a culture whose voices mostly champion individualism and not togetherness, the church needs to offer an alternative.

Finally, Christian community means that we share the difficult and tragic events of life. We grieve with and try to support people in families that break apart. We open our lives and homes to people with emotional difficulties who need a safe environment. We financially support people who can't afford the medications they need. We stand with and pray for healing for the member with a terminal illness. We struggle toward reconciliation when there is anger, betrayal, or frustration. In the end, through good and bad, thick and thin, we try to press on in life together.

Discipleship, Accountability, and a New Social Reality

Discipleship stands at the heart of Christian community. We do not build community primarily for emotional intimacy and social support—although we do experience those things in community. Rather, we build community primarily to follow Christ and to more faithfully and effectively allow God to reign in our lives. That is what makes these communities *Christian* ones and not just social clubs.

Christianity is a corporate as well as an individual faith. Becoming like Christ is a relational as well as personal process. For this reason, God calls believers to make their faith-journeys together, in small bands of people called "church." For our own well-being and growth, we need the benefit of each others' spiritual gifts, encouragements, role modeling, and challenges.

It is largely by sharing our lives in relationship together over time that God strengthens our faith, builds our character, and shapes us into the people we are meant to be. This makes sense, since most Christian virtues and fruits of the Spirit to which we are called—love, service, gentleness, humility, self-giving, patience, kindness, forgiveness—are expressed in relationships, not in isolation.

A key aspect of discipleship in Christian community is personal accountability. In community, we learn to be accountable. We learn, literally, to give an account to others. Accountability means that we can ask each other what is going on in our lives, how we are doing, or what is the state of our souls. And we can expect an honest answer.

Accountability also means that we can confront each other and be reconciled when we disappoint, anger, or hurt each other. Finally, accountability means that when we live irresponsibly or sinfully, we can admonish each other without fear of ruining our relationships.

Accountability in community rejects Lone Ranger Christianity. It repudiates privatized, individualistic faith. Accountability instead acknowledges our human and spiritual interdependence. It admits that our actions and attitudes affect each other deeply. We thus have a basic responsibility to each other.

Accountability recognizes that believers need each other's help and support in pursuing the kingdom of God. It knows we all have blind spots that others we know and trust can help us with. Being accountable means not saying "Mind your own business" but being instead willing to work through issues and problems until we reach unity and love.

Being held accountable is often difficult. Holding another accountable can be even harder. Accountability is unnatural for those of us raised in an individualistic, freedom-oriented, North American culture. Accountability is not an attempt to bully or police each other, however. It simply aims to build responsible, loving relationships in the context of Christian discipleship. Although accountability may not be quickly mastered, it *can* be learned through practice aided by God's grace and the community's support. And when accountability is exercised correctly, it is not a chore, but a deeply rewarding means to strengthen relationships and foster human growth.

In community, believers gradually relearn how to relate to each other according to the principles of the kingdom of God. They learn, for example, how to really love and serve each other in concrete ways, how to support each other in difficult times. They learn how to admonish and forgive each other for hurts or sins. They learn how to share their resources, and how together to minister God's mercy and love to broken people in a broken world.

Gradually, as believers learn these things, their communities develop distinct ways of life. They acquire particular patterns of social relations visibly different from those practiced by people in the larger world. The community then becomes a *new social reality* in which the kingdom of God is expressed, not only in the actions and attitudes of its individuals, but in the culture and social relations of a whole body of people.

By simply living out concrete, alternative social realities, informed by an alternative set of spiritual values, Christian communities witness to the breaking of the kingdom of

God into history. By simply being the people of God in this way, communities stand as concrete signs that God is indeed transforming this world by his love and mercy.

Hence, living in Christian community is both a necessary means for pursuing Christian discipleship *and* the natural result of a body of people shaping their lives according to God's kingdom. Christian community is, in this sense, both the path and the destination for believers.

A Word of Caution: First Things First

Many people go into Christian community with great dreams. That makes sense. Big dreams go with the territory. People who want more than what traditional churches offer, who can't abide our culture's individualism, who want to create an alternative way of life *must* be people of great dreams. These dreamers are important. They are exactly what this world of failed ideals and mediocre Christianity needs.

But sometimes big dreams can bring big problems. The problems don't come when people live their lives together in pursuit of great dreams they cherish. The problems come when the great dreams people cherish get in the way of how they live their lives together.

Great dreams can give inspiration, direction, and meaning to how we live our lives. But they can also blind us to how we ought to live our lives here and now. Whether our dreams guide or blind us depends on whether we are willing to do first things first, to start with the basics.

One basic ingredient of Christian community is that what's most important about Christian community is *doing* it. There are many who dream of, theorize about, teach on, and discuss Christian community. Then there are those who actually live it. The latter is the smaller group. Dreams are only valuable if they inspire us to live them.

Talk is easy and dreams exciting. But doing community is another matter. And in the end—as with the kingdom of God in general (Matt. 21:28-32; James 1:22-24)—doing it is what really matters.

Another basic of Christian community is learning to be *responsible* to each other. We're talking nitty-gritty here. Showing up at meetings. Bringing vegetables to meals when you're scheduled to. Letting people know about scheduling changes. The more our lives are intertwined, the more we affect each other, and the more we need to be responsible to each other in basic ways.

My home church rotates its meetings between a number of houses. Recently we decided to change the rotation schedule. Unfortunately, we all forgot to tell a family who was away when we made the decision. Their home was supposed to have been next. When the time came we all assembled for house church—all except that family.

Eventually one of us called them. "Hey, where are you?"

Puzzled, they answered, "We just spent the day cleaning the house for tonight's meeting. Where are you?"

Gulp.

These kinds of things are bound to happen. We *will* fail each other. Still, we can make a difference in *how often* and *how badly* we fail each other. Too much irresponsibility in the little things suggests we really don't care about or respect those we hurt. That ruins relationships—even between those who share the greatest dreams.

Learning to be responsible to other people does not mean learning to be responsible *for* them. Quite the contrary. We must take responsibility *for ourselves*. And so must everyone else.

Intertwining our lives in Christian community does not mean that we become each other's parents or that what happens in our lives is someone else's fault. It does not mean we have the right to drag everyone else through the mud of our chronic problems. If community is to work, we must all take responsibility for our own choices, our own growth, our own problems.

This does not produce the individualistic environment that, at first glance, one might expect. On the contrary, it is only by taking responsibility for ourselves that we can begin to act responsibly toward others. How can I treat other people responsibly if I do not take the responsibility myself to grow spiritually, to deal with my problems head-on, to actually show up at meetings on time? A community of people who do not take responsibility for themselves quickly becomes a mess of dependency and manipulation (which quickly—and rightly—breaks up)

The next basic of Christian community is learning to *love* and continue to love each other. It is easy to love our dreams about community. It is much harder to love the people with whom we do community. Sometimes in the life of Christian community we feel like saying, "Brother, I would die for you—just don't ask me to drive you to the auto shop *again*."

But loving real people, and not ideas about people, is what Christian community is about. If we don't do that, or at least learn to do it a little *better*, our dreams mean little.

Even harder, we need to learn *continuing* love. For the same old people. Sure, with some people the relational bonds grow stronger with each passing year. But with others, only irritation grows stronger. As in marriage, it's one thing to love when things are new and exciting. It can be quite another thing to love over the long haul.

Of course, it's axiomatic that most other people, when you really get to know them, are weird, neurotic, troublesome. But God calls us to love people as they are, not our unrealistic idealizations of them. Fortunately for us, God loves us and calls those other people to love *us* as we really are.

A basic building block of Christian community we have already touched on is learning *accountability* to each other. We need to learn both how to ask others for an account and how to give an account. If we can't do that, then we are living on parallel but separate tracks.

We must be clear about how we are and are not accountable to each other. As Christians, we are accountable to each other at the basic level of our walk before God as disciples of Jesus.

In intentional community, we are also accountable—obliged to be able to give an account—for commitments we have made. In my community, I am not accountable for failing to make a nice dinner for the folks next door. If they don't eat tonight, it's not my problem. Unless, of course, I signed up to bring them dinner because she just delivered a baby or he is sick. Then it *is* my problem. If I forget to do it, I am obliged to give an account (even if it's only "I'm sorry, I forgot"). All of this requires clarifying who is committed to whom for what.

Once we're clear about that, we must learn how to rightly call people to account. Clearly there are bad ways to do it ("Hey, you stupid jerk, where's the dinner you said you would bring?").

Then there are better ways ("You know, the person who organized the dinner list told me that you signed up for last night. Is that true or was there a mix-up?"). Most people know how to be tactful and polite—sometimes *so* polite we simply suppress our frustration, which won't do either.

Finally, we need to learn how to give an account to others when asked. Basic dangers here are defensiveness, resistance, withdrawal, or self-condemnation. But the goal is a short, honest, and frank discussion, characterized by understanding and forgiveness, which resolves the concern.

Christian community is made of basic stuff. People who don't worry about the little things because they are too preoccupied with the big things need to be turned on their heads—figuratively, and maybe literally. As the Scriptures teach, only those faithful in little things can ever really be faithful with big things.

Before we can achieve the impressive and inspiring, the stuff of big dreams, we need to get back to the basics. Seeking economic justice in the world only makes sense when we treat the people around us responsibly. Sharing the love of God with the world is only possible when we first love that pain-in-the-neck we see each week. To open ourselves to the Spirit's power to heal us involves taking responsibility for ourselves. Demonstrating peace and unity in Christ only works when we are accountable for and forgiving about what would otherwise divide us.

The proverb says, "Where there is no vision, the people perish" (Prov. 29:18, KJV). Great visions keep us moving forward and fill us with joyous anticipation. But another proverb, equally true, could be made: "Without the basics, our visions perish." Instead of cherishing great dreams which damage our life together, we need to live together in ways that bring to pass the great dreams we cherish.

Why Make Christian Community "Intentional"?

One final point. At this time in this culture, Christian community must be lived intentionally. It must be pursued consciously and purposefully. This is because the kind of community experience we are talking about does not happen by itself. If we want Christian community to happen, we must make it happen, we must *intend* it to happen.

Our culture and society do not generally encourage community—but individualistic autonomy. Geographical and social mobility keep people on the move. Careers often demand that people frequently change jobs and relocate. Few children settle where their parents lived.

Cars encourage people to spread out as they wish and commute to destinations. Hence members of a single church can easily live fifty or sixty miles apart. Modern society also fractures people's lives. Bits and pieces of time and energy are spent in disconnected yet demanding spheres of life—school, work, family, friends, church, clubs—without a framework unifying the whole of life.

Our culture often teaches us to make life choices which maximize our individual self-fulfillment and minimize any commitments and obligations which might constrain personal autonomy. Indeed, our political and cultural legacy emphasizes independence and teaches us not to let others interfere with whatever we consider our private business.

In this kind of social and cultural context, the ideas of Christian community—commitment, accountability, trust, personal openness, long-term relationships, and sacrifice—make little sense. Instead, it makes sense to think of church as a voluntary association we commute to. The church takes its place as one of modern life's fractures, which can be organized and run by the minister, which one searches out and joins. One then plugs in by attending meetings and functions as one is able, given life's other demands. Commitments should not be too demanding, because one may need to leave. On such occasions, goodbyes can be said and a new church found.

This is the kind of church that makes sense in our culture. Consequently, this is, in fact, the kind of church life many Christians experience and come to like.

Christians who want to live out the community to which the Bible calls them will thus have to do it consciously and intentionally. They will have to understand that in this society Christian community is an alien, alternative reality that must be purposefully pursued and cultivated. Without clear, conscious expectations, members of such a community can experience serious misunderstandings and hurts. But with clear purpose and intentionality, Christian community *can* be built.

Some Christian communities prepare written covenants as a specific way of being intentional. These are documents which objectively describe the kind of relationships these bodies are committed to. Written covenants cannot guarantee loving, community relationships. But they can make clear the relational expectations of the church community for newcomers. They can also remind long-standing members of their own tradition and vision.

The community I belong to, for example, has a written description of our covenant relationships. It describes how we as a body covenant together to forgive, pursue discipleship, pray, be available, serve, build strong relationships, be accountable. By writing down these goals and expectations of each other, we remind ourselves that achieving our biblical calling will not automatically happen. It will require real commitment and work.

At the same time, we must remember that community can be cultivated but not engineered. As Dietrich Bonhoeffer so clearly perceived, community is a gift, not a possession. It is a living, dynamic experience that is nurtured, not a prepackaged program that is instituted.

Still we can cultivate the fertile soil community needs. We can start, for example, simply by spending more time together, outside of "church," doing ordinary and extraordinary things. We can begin to pull down pretenses and defenses, to share our true selves with each other. We can learn to resolve interpersonal conflicts in constructive ways, and to stick with people who are different and difficult. In these and other ways, with God's grace and with the help of groups more experienced in such matters, the gift of Christian community can begin to grow and lead to basic, life-generating church renewal.

2

Do Church Without Clergy

I KNOW someone who recently left the clergy. He's happier now. Before he left, he was supposedly just one of a group of church elders, paid to preach and teach. Actually, however, this man was expected to do it all. He was to preach twice every Sunday, visit all the sick, oversee the secretary and youth leader, counsel all the troubled members, go to denominational meetings, conduct weddings, even stay late to lock the church doors.

Despite the church's official nonhierarchical theology, this pastor's position made him, in reality, the center of organization. He was the authority in decisions, the initiator of pastoral action, and the receiver of all complaints. He was *"The* Pastor." Something was wrong. He knew it. But he could do little to change things, because his congregation resisted change. Then he got another job offer.

Ministry is at the heart of church life. Ministry has to be done right for a church to be healthy and alive. Radical church renewal demands a transformed understanding and practice of ministry in the church. It calls us to shift ministry away from professionals and give it back to the ordinary people of God. To do this, we must rethink a key aspect of modern church life: the clergy.

The clergy seems an overrated institution. Many Christians assume, for example, that the most important aspect to consider in choosing a church is its minister. Christians tend to think a church cannot function effectively without a priest or pastor, that the first thing one must do in starting a church is to hire a minister to lead it. They believe Sunday morning should be judged by its sermon. They think the ordained, full-time Christian minister has answered God's highest call.

Could it be that clergy are neither necessary nor, in the long run, good for church? Is it possible that one of the best things that could happen to the church would be for the clergy to resign and take secular jobs?

These suggestions may seem absurd. Yet going to the root helps us see that our clergy system is not demanded by the New Testament. It is often counterproductive. And it can obstruct healthy, biblical church life.

We do need ministry, even some kinds of paid ministry. It is possible to structure the professional clergy to try to minimize its weaknesses and maximize its strengths. There are congregations with paid ministers which manage to also nurture the active, dynamic involvement of all congregational members for the common good.

But many others have made the case for the clergy. Here we want to explain why we may not need the clergy.

The Problem: Not People But the Profession

When we talk about clergy we are not referring to *the actual people* who are clergy. The specific men and women who are priests, ministers, and pastors are mostly wonderful people. They love and want to serve God. They want to serve the people of God. They typically are sincere, compassionate, intelligent, self-giving, and long-suffering. The problem with clergy is not the people who are clergy but the *profession* these people belong to.

Let it also be clear that clergy do much good in the church. It's not that clergy don't help people. They do—which is one reason they are such a dominant feature of church life. But the fact that clergy are doing lots of good for the church often means the people of God are not. We'll get back to that idea shortly.

Without a doubt, the clergy is a profession, and members of the clergy are professionals. Just as lawyers protect and interpret the law and doctors control and administrate medicine, clergy protect, interpret, and administrate the truth of God. This profession, like any profession, dictates standards of conduct for how its members should dress, speak, and act. Like other professions, it dictates standards of education, preparation, admittance to the profession, procedures for job searches, and retirement.

Clearly, Catholic priests and Protestant ministers alike are expected—by parishioners, friends, hierarchies, denominational authorities, and themselves—to have a distinct kind of training. They are to be certain kinds of people and perform certain kinds of duties. Some clergy even have their own professional title: Reverend.

Traditionally, the profession has demanded that clergy be male. Protestants have preferred that ministers be married—and happily so. The profession demands that its members possess a seminary degree and official ordination credentials. The profession requires that clergy be extraordinarily (and unrealistically) gifted. They are to be natural leaders, skilled orators, capable administrators, compassionate counselors, wise decision makers, dispassionate conflict resolvers, and astute theologians.

Clergy function essentially as professional church managers. They are responsible for preparing teachings, homilies, and sermons; visiting the sick; conducting funerals and marriages; properly administering the sacraments. They oversee church social events, Sunday school, and catechism programs. They must prepare engaged couples for marriage and counsel anyone with problems. They prepare denominational reports, attend denominational meetings, manage missionary and evangelistic programs.

They assemble and oversee staff, such as assistant ministers, youth group leaders, administrative staffs, and evangelism teams. They organize fundraising drives. They attend to community relations, facilities use, building maintenance. They encourage, discipline, and edify parishioners. They establish the vision of the church.

There exists, then, a definite set of tasks which everyone (even the non-Christian) knows are rightful clergy duties. Everyone knows this because the clergy is a formally institutionalized profession, created and maintained by denominations, hierarchies, seminaries, the laity, and, finally, the clergy themselves.

The New Testament Vision: Ministry by the Entire Body

To grasp the value of church without clergy, we need to remind ourselves of the biblical vision of ministry in the church. The New Testament is clear that ministry in the church is the work of the entire body of believers, not of a single minister or pastoral team. Church ministry is not the domain of hierarchies and professionals. Rather, the church is to find its life in ministry through the active contribution of each member's gifts.

The vision is simple: the church is a living body which needs to be strengthened and matured. The Spirit of God gives gifts to each member of the body. "But to each one is given the manifestation of the Spirit for the common good" (1 Cor. 12:7, NASB; also see Eph. 4:7).

God gives these gifts to all so each member can participate in building up the faith and life of the church. "What is the outcome then, brethren? When you assemble, each one has a psalm, has a teaching, has a revelation, has a tongue, has an interpretation. Let all things be done for edification" (1 Cor. 14:26, NASB; also see Eph. 4:12).

For the church to function properly, all members must fully, actively, and responsibly participate and contribute their gifts. Paul explains to the believers in Rome,

> Just as each of us has one body with many parts, and these parts do not all have the same function, so in Christ we who are many form one body, and each part belongs to all the others. We have different gifts according to the grace given us. If a person's gift is prophesying, let them use it in proportion to their faith. If it is serving, let them serve; if teaching, let them teach; if encouraging, let them encourage; if it is contributing to the needs of others, let them give generously; if it is giving aid, let them do so diligently; if showing mercy, let them do it cheerfully. (Rom. 12:4-8, author's paraphrase)

Each member has important pieces of the church's "ministry puzzle," so to speak. Without everyone's contribution, that puzzle is full of holes.

In Paul's mind, certain spiritual gifts are especially important because of their contribution to the entire body's ability to minister. These include apostleship, prophesy, evangelism, pastoring, and teaching (Eph. 4:11; 1 Cor. 12:28). But the fact that these are especially valuable gifts does not mean that they should be separated out and labeled "*The* Ministry."

Quite the opposite. These gifts exist precisely to facilitate the ministry *of everyone else* in the church, "to prepare God's people for works of ministry, so that the body of Christ might be built up" (Eph. 4:12, author's paraphrase). Thus even though some gifts are key, the work of ministry in the church belongs to all the saints.

Ordinary believers can be ministers because, in the new covenant, all the people of God are a holy priesthood. "You . . . are being built into a spiritual house to be a holy priesthood. . . . You are a chosen people, a royal priesthood" (1 Pet. 2:5, 9, NIV). Jesus has made all the saints "to be a kingdom and priests to serve his God and Father" (Rev. 1:6, NIV; also see Rev. 10:12, 19:22).

Many reformers, like Luther, theologized about the priesthood of all believers. But few actually carried this radical theology to its rightful conclusions. Few created church structures that really equipped all the people to minister. And those that did have often drifted back into the old priesthood-of-some-believers mentality.

The New Testament vision of ministry thus does not conceive of the church as a formal institution that needs to be managed and directed. That is the modern, corporate business model, for which people get MBAs. Rather, the church is a living organism that needs each of its parts to work toward the whole body's health (1 Cor. 12:12-27; Rom. 12:4-5; Eph. 4:16).

The less visible and impressive parts of the body are no more dispensable than the others (1 Cor. 12:20-25). And again, every member's active participation is absolutely necessary to keep the body healthy. In other words, a biblical church is a participatory society, a people's church.

To better understand the New Testament approach to ministry, it is helpful to recall the reason why Christians ought to gather for church in the first place. The central purpose of church is not necessarily worship and praise. Although believers clearly ought to worship God, the

New Testament's description of church gatherings hardly addresses praise and worship. Instead, the Bible understands worship as something which should characterize the whole of our lives (Rom. 12:1). Neither is missions the central purpose of gathering as Christians. According to the New Testament, what goes on in church meetings is primarily for the benefit of the ones gathered who are *already* believers.

The central purpose of church is not only worship and not missions, but mutual edification, the building up of the church's members through ministry to each other. Notice how, in his most extended discussion of church life, the apostle Paul continually emphasizes edification as the chief goal of church gatherings (1 Cor. 14:3-5, 12, 17, 26; also see Rom. 14:19; Eph. 4:12, 29). Christians, Paul argues, should meet to build each other up. "When you assemble . . . let all things be done for edification" (1 Cor. 14:26, NASB). And edification, we've seen, is the active participation of every member of the body in decentralized, mutual ministry.

But Why Church Without Clergy?

But what about full-time church ministry? Even many advocates of the clergy profession agree with this vision of decentralized church ministry. They just think that as part of the model, churches should also hire trained, ordained, full-time ministers. So, why should churches consider eliminating their clergy? Here are reasons.

First, the Bible does not require or command hiring full-time ministers. It is not something churches *have* to do.

Second, even if churches *choose* to hire paid ministers, which they may, there is not strong biblical support for the choice. Such a decision must be based more on practical and pragmatic than biblical grounds.

Third, however, when we honestly consider the actual, practical, pragmatic effects of professional ministry, we see that the clergy system unintentionally subverts the biblical model of church ministry described above. On the purely practical level of actual outcomes, the clergy system works against the participatory ministry of the body.

In any case, fourth, there is a world of difference between the paid ministries the New Testament briefly mentions and the kind of work professional clergy regularly perform. Even if the New Testament allows or encourages some forms of paid church ministry, what the New Testament has in mind is different from what most clergy actually are trained and expected to do.

Finally, the radical alternative—church without clergy—is a structure which does facilitate the New Testament vision of ministry. By de-professionalizing ministry, we can create the space and necessity for all God's people to minister.

In short, there is no biblical requirement for professional church ministry and many pragmatic reasons not to have professional church ministry. Let me elaborate.

The New Testament on Paid Ministry

Many Christians often assume the Bible *obliges* churches to hire full-time ministers. The New Testament does in a few places mention paying ministers for their work. But when we study these passages, we actually find meager support for hiring professional ministers in the church.

In the key passages on spiritual gifts, we see that there are many ministries of God's people. They range from healing to teaching, serving to giving money, evangelism to having great faith in trying circumstances, working miracles to showing mercy (1 Cor. 12:4-11; Rom. 12:4-8; Eph. 4:11-12).

In Paul's mind, the list of gifts is open-ended and as endless as God is generous. Some people think some of these gifts, like teaching, deserve payment. Nothing in these passages tells us that, however. Nothing in the description of these gifts indicates that any of these are formal offices which a hired professional must fill. Thus creating the single, formal office of *the* preacher, based on these passages, is no more justified than creating the formal offices of mercy shower, exhorter, or money giver. Biblical support for paid ministry must be found elsewhere.

What about 1 Corinthians 9:1-18? At first glance, the evidence seems clear. "The Lord has commanded that those who preach the gospel should receive their living from the gospel" (v. 14, NIV). On close inspection, however, the evidence becomes ambiguous.

Interestingly, Paul's real point here is to argue *against* his being paid for ministry. Indeed, Paul claims that he would rather "put up with anything" (v. 12, NIV) and "would rather die" (v. 15, NIV) than accept financial support from the Corinthians. In his judgment, receiving money for his work would likely "hinder the gospel of Christ" (v. 12, NIV).

More importantly, in this passage Paul is not discussing whether to pay teachers or elders in the Corinthian or any other church. Rather, Paul is discussing the financial support of the ministry of *apostles* (*apo*: "from," *stellō*: "to send"), those sent out to evangelize nonbelievers and plant churches. There is an important difference between the two.

In Paul's mind, his special apostolic work *to* churches was quite different in purpose and operation from the regular exercise of gifts by believers *within* the churches he planted. For example, the goal of church ministry was primarily inward-directed-edification toward maturity. But the goal of the work of apostles was outwardly, toward evangelistic church planting.

There were other differences between the ministry of apostles and other believers. First, ministry within churches was fixed in specific geographic locations. But the work of apostles was, by definition, on the road. We see this in Jesus' original sending of the apostles (Matt. 10:1-14), in Paul's many missionary journeys, and in the fact that the other apostles' wives had to be taken along (1 Cor. 9:5, NIV).

Second, ministry within churches was ongoing, but the work of apostles was time-limited—once Paul planted a church, he soon moved on.

1 Corinthians 9 does teach that the itinerant, missionary work of *apostles* deserved to be funded by other believers, today as much as in Paul's time. This makes sense. Evangelistic church planters normally need external financial support, since working a steady job is difficult for someone on the road.

But 1 Corinthians 9 does not teach that the ongoing exercise of spiritual gifts within an existing church should be salaried. That is a different idea altogether, one quite foreign to both of Paul's letters to the Corinthian believers. Thus, if people we call clergy are to be paid, 1 Corinthians 9 does not finally address the matter (and the same reasoning applies to 2 Cor. 11:8-9 and Phil. 4:15-18).

In Matthew 10:5-10 and Luke 9:1-5, Jesus sent out the twelve disciples to preach without any money, for, he says, "the worker is worth his keep" (Matt. 10:10, NIV; cf. Lev. 19:13; Deut. 24:14-15; Luke 10:3-7). Does this sanction paid ministry in the church? Not really. Again, this was not a ministry within established churches. Churches had not even been established! Rather, the twelve, like Paul, were being commissioned and sent by Jesus as *apostles* to *evangelize* (Luke 9:2).

Finally, we come to 1 Timothy 5:17-18, the only passage

which seems to directly address paid, non-apostolic ministry *in the church*.

> Consider the elders who care for the church well worthy of double honor, especially those whose work is preaching and teaching. For the Scripture says: "Do not muzzle the ox while it is treading out grain," and "The worker is worth his wages." (Author's paraphrase)

This is the most straightforward New Testament passage on paid ministry. Yet even the meaning of these verses is somewhat ambiguous.

Verse 17 alone, without the qualification of verse 18, would say nothing about paying money to ministers in the church. The common Greek word for "payment" is *misthos*. But this is not the word Paul uses to describe what the elders deserve—even though he does use *misthos* in the very next verse. Nor does Paul use any of the available words for "money" (*argurion, chrēma, chalkos, kerma, nomisma*).

Instead, Paul only claims that these elders are worthy of double honor (*time*). This means exactly what it says: social esteem. Thus, were it not for the qualification of verse 18, no one would have ever thought to interpret this as evidence for paid church ministry. Nonetheless, it is likely Paul had some form of monetary payment in mind. For the two Old Testament passages in verse 18 are quoted by both Jesus and Paul elsewhere in reference to financial support (Luke 10:7; 1 Cor. 9:9).

One interpretation is that those elders who preach and teach especially well should, indeed, be given double honor. The first honor is esteem, and the second financial payment. This interpretation remains speculative, of course, and should not be pressed too hard.

Even if we assume 1 Timothy 5 advocates paying preachers and teachers, questions remain. What kind of financial payment? How often? How much? This we cannot exactly know. But Paul's word choice indicates that probably he wanted the elders to be periodically compensated for their work with *honoraria*. If, beyond that, they were drawing regular, full time salaries, nothing in this passage says so.

Thus the New Testament actually offers only limited support for having paid ministry in the church. By extension of the apostolic principle, evangelistic church planters merit financial support. Two verses do suggest that teachers and preachers receive honoraria for their work. This is hardly overwhelming *biblical* ground on which to build the dominating clergy profession that has become a central feature of church life today. In addition, even though the New Testament does speak of some form of paid church ministry, what the New Testament seems to have in mind is very different from our view of clergy as professions who run the church.

What About Pragmatic Reasons?

Of course, we need not necessarily be limited by the New Testament. Contemporary churches need not see the meager New Testament support for paid leadership as forbidding the practice. Just because the early church didn't do it doesn't mean we can't.

Following this reasoning, some people argue that even if there are not solid *biblical* grounds for paid ministry, there are compelling *pragmatic* grounds. They argue that in today's society everyone is so busy and their work so specialized that the only way to guarantee good preaching and pastoral work in church is to hire a trained specialist.

It is true we don't have to mimic the early churches. We are free to develop our church practices in ways beyond those specified by the New Testament. But if the Bible is in any sense an authority for us, we are only free to do this so long as what we develop is at least compatible with and thus does not violate what the New Testament does teach.

The problem with the clergy system is that there is usually a large gap between the *abstract* theologies about what clergy are and the empirical reality of what clergy *actually* are. In the real world, the clergy system often violates the New Testament vision of church ministry, even if unintentionally. How does this happen?

The Clergy Profession Fosters Passive Laity

God intends church to be a community of believers in which each member ministers by contributing special gifts to the whole. Through the active participation and contribution of all, the church is built up. The church is to be a body, with each unique, necessary part working for the good of the whole. Without each member contributing, the body becomes lame (1 Cor. 12:20-25).

Sadly, the actual effect of the clergy profession is often to make the body of Christ lame. This happens not because clergy intend it but because the profession so easily turns the laity into passive receivers.

The clergy role centralizes and professionalizes the gifts of the whole body into one person. In this way, the clergy system represents Christianity's capitulation to modern society's tendency toward specialization. Clergy are spiritual specialists, church specialists. Thus the multitude of spiritual gifts which belong to all are centralized and vested in a special caste of Christians. Other Christians become merely ordinary believers who hold secular jobs. They specialize in non-spiritual activities such as plumbing, teaching, or marketing.

Since the pastor is paid to be the specialist in church operations and management, the laity understandably begin to assume a passive role in church. Rather than fully contributing their part to edify the church, they become passive receivers expecting edification. Rather than actively spending time and energy exercising their gift for the good of the body, they sit back and let the pastor run the show.

Think about Sunday morning. Parishioners arrive on schedule and sit quietly in pews. They watch and listen to the minister who is up front, center stage, his or her presence dominating the service. They stand, sit, speak, and sing only when directed to by the minister or the program. Yet what happens during this hour on Sunday morning is only a microcosmic picture of the whole church reality.

In the end, the church becomes a formal association in which rank-and-file members belong by paying dues and attending meetings. It becomes an association organized, guided, and governed by a professional leader or administrative bureaucracy. Hardly the New Testament vision of church.

Suppose the people of a congregation were to grasp the vision that the church is not a formal association but a community. That gifts are distributed to each person. That everyone must actively participate and contribute for church to work. That no one's gifts are more spiritual than another's. That everyone's participation will ensure a full, healthy church life. Then many might reasonably ask themselves, "Why are we paying our pastor?"

Professional ministers are needed when church members are not doing their part. But when all church members are actively participating and fully making their contribution for the good of the body, clergy are unnecessary. That is a new thought for many. But it is a fact proven every day in the experience of countless Christian communities and home churches around the world.

The Clergy Profession Fosters Dependent Laity

The clergy profession is self-defeating. Its stated purpose is to nurture spiritual maturity in the church. A valuable goal. In actuality, however, it often accomplishes the opposite, nurturing a permanent dependence of laity on clergy. While intending to empower, the clergy profession often disempowers. Clergy come to resemble parents whose children never grow up, therapists whose clients never become healed, teachers whose students never graduate.

I know of a church which fired its pastor because, in the congregation's judgment, he did not visit members at home often enough. What kind of mentality could do this? Only one which assumes it is the pastor's job to do everything. Only one which has forgotten that the saints of God have the ability and responsibility to minister to each other. Only one which has no clue about the New Testament vision of the ministry of the saints.

Yet this kind of mentality pervades the churches today. In churches all over the country, the people of God end up thinking and saying things like, "That's a good idea, but we better get the okay of pastor Bob first." And "Those new people are causing real trouble in our church. When is Reverend John going to do something about it?"

This dependence is then construed as evidence of the necessity for professionalized ministry. The circle is vicious. The laity cannot make it on their own; they obviously need a full-time minister. But that dependency is to a significant degree a product of the clergy system. Using the cause of the trouble to solve it is like treating the flu with more flu virus.

I have often heard clergy talk about the need to work themselves out of their jobs. But it seems rarely to happen. Gradualism is not the answer. The clergy system is too deeply ingrained. So is the passivity and dependence it produces. If congregations are to wake up and get back on track, the solution will have to be more radical.

The Clergy Profession is Unrealistically Demanding of Clergy

That the clergy system fosters passivity and dependence is trouble enough. But there is another problem—what the clergy system does to the people in the profession. Being a member of the modern clergy is difficult. When good-hearted men and women pour their lives into the task they often encounter stress, frustration, and burnout. It's no wonder, of course, since clergy are trying to do the work of a whole congregation by themselves!

In the Corinthian church, apparently everyone wanted to be the same part of the body (1 Cor. 12:12-20). So Paul asked the obvious question, "if everyone were only one body part, where would the rest of the body be?" (1 Cor. 12:19, author's paraphrase).

Our clergy system inverts this distortion. Instead of everyone trying to be and do only one thing, we expect only one person to be and do all things. But how can a single person be a skilled leader, orator, visionary, administrator, counselor, decision maker, conflict resolver, and theologian?

What we expect of professional ministers is as unrealistic as would be a corporation's demands that a single employee fill or oversee all corporate roles, from mailboy to secretary to middle manager to president. Meanwhile most other employees would show up one day a week to admire the super-employee (and sometimes do a chore the super-employee asked them to do).

The clergy profession demands super-Christian, super-human accomplishment. Christians—with our realistic understanding of human limitations and weaknesses—

should know better. God certainly did, which is why God made maintaining and building the church the shared responsibility of *all* believers.

I know of a church which spent three years searching for the perfect pastor. After one year of ministry, the pastor confessed to having an adulterous relationship and stepped down. The problem was not that this congregation accidentally chose the wrong person. Nor was the problem that the pastor was more sinful than the rest of us.

Such problems grow out of the professionalized clergy role itself. Congregations place unrealistically high demands and expectations on a human being. By placing pastors on pedestals, congregations removed them from necessary channels of accountability and support. When will we learn?

Often individual ministers, who understand this, hope to make their role more realistic and biblical. But they eventually discover that, for the most part, they can't reshape the role at will because their congregations and denominations expect the standard things from them. Of course, that's the nature of social roles: they shape people more than people shape them.

The answer is not gradualism. It is decisive, structural change. It is church without clergy. The goal is simply to create in churches the space and the necessity for all the ordinary people of God to exercise their gifts for the good of the body. Without the clergy, churches will face two options: sink or swim. And it is amazing how well the people of God can swim when, in fact, they have a reason to.

Answering Some Questions

Pondering church without clergy raises big questions which deserve consideration.

For example, doesn't the New Testament command

churches to have elders? Not exactly. In fact, some New Testament churches, (in Crete, Ephesus, and Phillipi, for example) had elders. Others, (in Rome, Corinth, Galatia) apparently did not. Furthermore, Paul hardly ever addressed elders in his letters. Instead, he usually wrote to all the members of churches, because *they* were the most important ministers of the church.

Finally, where elders did exist in the New Testament, the role they played bears little resemblance to our contemporary clergy role. They were simply groups of older, wiser members whose strong Christian character placed them in a good position to watch over the church. They were certainly *not* a professional class paid to run the church.

We may, like the New Testament churches, choose to have groups of elders. But that is an entirely different issue than whether it makes sense to have clergy.

Another question. Doesn't the Levitical priestly class in the Old Testament offer a model of worship and ministry which should carry over into the new covenant? Absolutely. The New Testament model is perfectly clear: in the new covenant, *all* believers become priests before God (1 Pet. 2:5, 9; Rev. 1:6). And as priests, we all offer up *new* kinds of sacrifices (Rom. 12:1; Phil. 2:17; Phil. 4:18; Heb. 13:15-16). Other than this, the New Testament knows nothing of a special priestly class distinct from the laity.

But without clergy, who will preach? The New Testament answer is clear again. All those members who have the gift of preaching and teaching should preach and teach. Verbal instruction and proclamation of the Word are crucial aspects of church life. That is why churches should benefit from *all* the teaching gifts in the church.

Most churches actually possess many members with the gifts of preaching and teaching, although they may not realize it. The clergy system, however, assumes that each church has one and only one person with those gifts—and even they must usually be hired from outside! Under the clergy system, all the other teaching gifts in the body sit idly in the pew, perpetually atrophied and neglected. Meanwhile, the congregation hears only from one preacher week after week, like a family eating the same food for dinner every night.

Churches need good teaching. We should train people for it and, if necessary, even pay them for it—although with more than one teacher and a broader understanding of what teaching can be, it hardly needs to be a full-time job. But churches do not need the clergy profession to have good teaching. In fact, church without clergy can actually enhance and enrich teaching and preaching in the church by drawing on and cultivating all gifts in the body.

One implication of this, by the way, is that we need to reconceive the role of seminaries and training for the ministry. Formal biblical, theological, and pastoral education has a place. But it should not be to train a clerical class of professional Christians. Rather, seminaries and theology schools should be oriented toward equipping all the people of God to exercise their gifts. In other words, seminaries should gear their programs and courses to training non-professionals to be ministers according to their gifts.

But without clergy, won't many church programs come to a screeching halt? Yes, which is exactly what most institutional churches need! A multitude of church programs is not the solution. Usually it is part of the problem. Radical church renewal means cutting back on programmed, churchy busyness. It means building instead relationships in community and learning to minister to each other. It is amazing how many "important" church programs can be eliminated, without real loss.

On the other hand, those core programs that really *are* important will be maintained by the people, precisely because the body finds them to be valuable. The rest can fall by the wayside. So much the better.

But won't many churchgoers today simply refuse to spend the time and effort to participate and contribute their gifts? Christian community and church without clergy are demanding—more demanding than many people are willing to live with. If they don't have a pastor to do it for them, they may drop out of church. What then?

Perhaps let them leave. Might it be better for everyone if we had small, committed, responsible, and active congregations—rather than large ones wanting the convenience of paying to be taken care of? Church renewal is not forged by lukewarm, passive, demanding people. Besides, when churches get straightened out, perhaps these people will return and change their ways. In any case, without a professional pastor to pay, the loss in church revenue is not so threatening.

Is a vision of church without clergy an endorsement of strict egalitarianism, as if there were *no* differences in the church? No. Different members have different gifts which affect the church differently. We should recognize the differences and appreciate those gifts which are especially important (more on this in the next chapter). But we don't need to professionalize and pay for the exercise of gifts.

But without clergy, who will conduct weddings? If many churches are not entirely clear on the New Testament view of ministry in the church, the state is even less clear. Hence, the state demands that weddings be conducted by ordained persons. From a biblical perspective, there is nothing magical about ordination for weddings (in fact, there is nothing magical about ordination at all). The simple solution to this problem is simply commissioning whoever in the church is going to officiate at the wedding by laying hands on them. This simple and natural procedure satisfies all the state's ordination requirements.

Finally, in a church without clergy, who has authority, who disciplines, who makes decisions? Those questions will be answered in the next chapter.

Christian Truth Is Not That Fragile

In Christ there are no special distinctions, classes, or elites—we are all brothers and sisters in the family of God (Matt. 23:8). Nevertheless, human societies throughout history have consistently created spiritual castes of people—shamans, priests, soothsayers, witch doctors, wise men, prophets, gurus. The Christian church has been no exception. It didn't take long for the church to construct (based on a handful of ambiguous and misinterpreted Scripture verses) a massive, institutional, hierarchical superstructure. This created the two-class, authoritarian system of clergy versus laity.

Protestants broke with the Catholic Church, of course. But Protestants are as "Catholic" as Roman Catholics when it comes to clergy. Although the Bible replaced the sacraments as the center of God's revelation for Protestants, the profession they set up to protect and distribute this revelation is functionally similar to the Catholic priesthood. As the priest correctly administers the wafer, the minister correctly interprets the Word of God.

The clergy are the keepers of the church. But the church doesn't need to be kept by clergy. *God* keeps the church and asks all believers to participate in keeping it. Clergy professionals are to preserve, protect, and dispense Christian truth, correct teachings, the Bible, the sacraments, and authority. Yet truth is not so fragile it needs such care.

Christian truth is not some classified or dangerous material which only card-carrying experts can handle. Nor is it like riches which need the protection of safe vaults and armed security guards. It is the Holy Spirit's, not the hierarchy or denomination's job, to preserve Christian truth in history. And the Holy Spirit has preserved truth by distributing it to all of the people of God so they can share it together. As John taught, "You have an anointing from the Holy One, and all of you know the truth. . . . The anointing you received from him remains in you, and you do not need anyone to teach you" (1 John 2:20, 27, NIV).

Radical church renewal calls us to choose church without clergy, to end this conspicuous and ingrained feature of church life which has little biblical justification. Pastors themselves need liberation from demands that they be ultraversatile, multitalented, superhuman performers And lay people need to be jarred from the pacifying illusion that, if they didn't go to seminary and aren't paid by the church, they need only attend church and tithe.

Church without clergy is hardy. It demands the full, active participation of everyone. It demands that we restructure our schedules and commitments around the biblical vision of ministry rather than the constraints of modern society. But the rewards of church without clergy—the renewed riches of participation, solidarity, and growth—make the effort exceedingly worthwhile.

3

Decentralize Leadership and Decision Making

(This chapter was written with Hal Miller.)

A NUMBER of years ago I attended a city council hearing. It concerned a homeless shelter a local church had started in its basement. The church's neighbors wanted the shelter closed because, they argued, the shelter was lowering their property values. But the church's pastor was a dynamic, commanding person. As far as he was concerned, the shelter was staying.

In the middle of the hearing, a member of the church stood. Her eyes were bitter; her body language revealed rage. She told in detail how she and her husband opposed the shelter, how they had argued against it in church meetings, and how the church was railroaded into hosting the shelter by headstrong leaders.

The longer she spoke, the more uncomfortable I became. I didn't know who was right or wrong. But I felt sad that the church had to air its dirty laundry publicly. Couldn't the matter have been handled differently?

Beyond that, the hearing raised many questions in my mind about the proper place of authority, decision making, leadership, and unity in the church. Who should lead the church? Who should have authority? Who ought to make decisions and how should they make them? These are major questions for churches in the process of radical renewal, especially for churches without clergy.

Leadership and Authority in the New Testament

Radical church renewal seeks to transform the contemporary church according to principles of church life found in the Bible. The goal is not to *imitate* the first-century church, for our modern social reality is different from the first century. The goal is rather to create a church experience that is both true to biblical principles of church life *and* appropriate for our modern context.

But our ideas of what the Bible says about church life are often clouded and distorted by human traditions and customs, especially when it comes to authority and leadership. Thus it is helpful to read the Bible with new eyes. What we discover is often surprising.

The most striking thing about the New Testament stance on church authority and leadership is how little it says about such issues. This is the opposite of what one would expect from the Bible, given that issues of authority and leadership dominate so many churches.

Jesus had little to say about church organization. He did declare that Peter, as representative of the apostles (or perhaps Peter's confession itself) would be the foundation upon which he would build the church (Matt. 16:18). Jesus also commanded his followers, when they met together, to eat a meal in memory of him (Luke 22:19-20). And Jesus gave the church authority to discipline sinners (Matt. 18:17).

Jesus criticized the Pharisees for their pretentious domination. He commanded his disciples, "Do not be called rabbi; for one is your master, and you are all brothers. . . . And do not be called leaders; for one is your leader, that is, Christ" (Matt. 23:8, 10, author's paraphrase). Jesus claimed that all authority in the universe had been transferred from all others to himself (Matt. 28:18). In response to his disciples' drive for authority to command, Jesus taught:

> You know that the rulers of the Gentiles lord it over them, and their great men exercise authority over them. It is not so among you, but whoever wishes to become great among you shall be your servant, and whoever wishes to be first among you shall be your slave. (Matt. 20:25-27, NASB; also see Luke 22:25-26; Matt. 23:11)

Thus if Jesus taught anything concerning leadership and authority among believers, it seems to have been egalitarianism.

But should not leaders have authority to rule the church? When we look further into the New Testament, we see that God, Jesus, the Holy Spirit, and various angels, demons, and "principalities and powers" have power (*dunamis*). Human beings are sometimes energized by these heavenly powers to perform miracles and live righteously. But the New Testament does not see humans as having power in their own right—it always comes from elsewhere.

In the New Testament God, Jesus, the Spirit, angels, and demons do have authority (*exousia*). Political leaders also have authority (Rom. 13:1-2). Jesus' disciples had authority over diseases and spirits (Matt. 10:1). Ananias and Sapphira had authority over their possessions (Acts 5:4). The apostles had authority to eat, drink, and become married (1 Cor. 9:4-5). Husbands and wives are seen to have mutual authority over their bodies (1 Cor. 7:4).

But never in the New Testament is one believer, even a church leader, said to have spiritual authority over another. Christians have authority over things, and even over spirits, but not over other Christians.

The single exception to this is 2 Corinthians 10:8 and 13:10. Here the apostle Paul speaks of having authority for building up and not destroying the Corinthian believers. Yet even here Paul's authority is not to be exercised *over* the Corinthians. It is to be used *for* a purpose: to build up the Corinthians.

Furthermore, Paul is, by his own admission, "speaking as a fool" (2 Cor. 11:17, 21, NIV). Elsewhere, when he speaks soberly, Paul studiously avoids claiming authority over other believers.

Finally, in this passage Paul goes to great lengths to persuade the Corinthians to listen to him. If he had authority over them, in the typical sense, why did he bother? Why did he not just give orders and end the discussion? The answer, we will see, is that any authority in the church is based on the ability to persuade with truth. It is not, as is often thought, rooted in the ability to coerce with force.

Take another angle. What or who does the New Testament say believers should obey (*hupakouō*)? Christians should obey God (Acts 5:29), Jesus (Matt. 28:20), the gospel (Rom. 10:16), and the teachings of the apostles (Phil. 2:12; 2 Thess. 3:14). Children should obey their parents and servants their masters (Eph. 6:1, 5).

But never are believers commanded to obey church leaders. Doesn't Heb. 13:17 say to obey church leaders, however? No. When rightly translated, Hebrews 13:17 does not say to "obey" (*hupakouō*) your leaders, but to "let yourself be persuaded by" (*peithō*, middle-passive form) your leaders. This is noteworthy. It is also reminiscent of the 2 Corinthians 10:8 and 13:10 passages. Christians are not to mindlessly obey leaders because they have the right to command—they don't. Rather, believers are to open themselves to be (in the course of ongoing exchanges and discussions) persuaded and convinced by leaders whom they know to speak the truth.

The second verb in Hebrews 13:17 reinforces this conclusion. Believers are not directed here to "submit" (*hupotassomai*) to their leaders. They are not, that is, to place themselves under the organizational authority of their leaders. Rather, they are instructed to "yield to" (*hupeikō*) their leaders, in the sense of retiring from a struggle or retreating from a battle. The idea is that, when necessary, Christians ought to give way to their leaders.

The New Testament specifically charges leaders *not* to lord it over believers. They are simply to rightly influence them by setting appealing examples with their own lives (1 Pet. 5:3). In return, church members should not arrogantly disregard nor mindlessly obey leaders. They should know, acknowledge, and appreciate (*oida*) those who lead and admonish in their churches (1 Thess. 5:12). Further, they ought to do this not because of their leaders' positions or supposed authority, but simply because of the value of their leaders' work (1 Thess. 5:13).

Thus the idea that church leaders are normally supposed to authoritatively rule or direct their churches seems unbiblical. Never in the New Testament are church leaders seen making decisions for the church without the involvement of the entire church. Indeed, in the case where the Jerusalem elders met over a major problem, it was "the apostles and elders, *with the whole church*," (emphasis added) that finally decided what to do (Acts 15:22, NIV). Furthermore, church leaders are normally not seen disciplining believers. Rather, God (1 Cor. 11:32; Heb. 12:5-11; Rev. 3:19) or the entire church (Matt. 18:17; 1 Cor. 5; Gal. 6:1-2) exercises discipline.

Only in the *extremely dangerous* situations of Ephesus and

Crete did Paul advocate that leaders discipline. There he took the emergency measure of sending Timothy and Titus to forcefully rebuke "men of depraved minds," whose teachings "spread like gangrene" (2 Tim. 3:8; 2 Tim. 2:17, NIV). In Ephesus, some believers had already "rejected and shipwrecked their faith" (1 Tim. 1:19, author's paraphrase). They had "turned away to follow Satan" (1 Tim. 5:15, NIV) and "wandered from the faith" (1 Tim. 6:21, author's paraphrase) and "from the truth" (2 Tim. 2:18, NIV). They had destroyed their faith (2 Tim. 2:18). In Crete, the false teachings of these "warped and sinful" men had already ruined "whole households" (Titus 3:11; 1:11, NIV). Clearly, the *very faith* of these churches was in jeopardy.

In these unusual circumstances, emergency measures, equal to the extreme dangers to faith, were necessary to oppose and rebuke these false teachers (see 1 Tim. 1:3-4; 4:1-2, 15-16; 2 Tim. 2:14-19; 3:1-9; 4:2-4, 14; Titus 1:10-16; 2:15; 3:10-11). These measures were desperate and unusual, not ones to characterize normal church life. Indeed, Paul himself studiously avoided such commanding of believers in the bad but not so dire circumstances of Corinth (1 Cor. 7:6; 2 Cor. 8:8). Furthermore, the people being disciplined were not really believers, but outside intruders.

Had New Testament church leaders ordinarily had special authority to command their churches, we would expect the epistles to have been written directly to them. Then the instructions given in the epistles could have been officially implemented by these leaders from above. But most of the epistles were written to all the believers of a church. They were addressed to "all in Rome" (Rom. 1:7), "the church of God in Corinth" (1 Cor. 1:2; 2 Cor. 1:1), "the churches in Galatia" (Gal. 1:2), "the saints in Ephesus" (Eph. 1:1), "all the saints in Christ Jesus at Philippi" (Phil. 1:1), "the holy and faithful brothers in

Christ at Colosse" (Col. 1:2), "to the church of the Thessalonians" (1 Thess. 1:1; 2 Thess. 1:1, all references NIV). And the list could go on (James 1:1; 1 Pet. 1:1; 2 Pet. 1:1; 1 John 2:1,7; Jude 1:1). Hebrews actually seems to have been written specifically *not* to leaders. The author had to ask the readers to greet their leaders for them (Heb 13:24).

Of the few epistles not written to all believers, only those to Timothy and Titus—who were dealing with emergency situations—carried instructions they were to implement as "missionary troubleshooters." The others (Philem., 2 John, 3 John) deal with personal matters between the author and the person addressed.

Biblical translators (with their own assumptions about church authority) often mistranslate the Greek into authority-oriented English language. For example, 1 Timothy 5:17 is often translated to indicate that elders "direct" and "rule over" the church. However, a more accurate translation has elders "taking the lead in caring for" (*proistēmi*) the church. This emphasizes a more serving, nurturing role of elders.

Similarly, 1 Thessalonians 5:12 is often translated that Christians should "respect" church leaders. A more accurate translation, however, is simply that we should "know" or "recognize" (*oida*) church leaders.

In typical translations of Acts 14:23, Paul and Barnabas "appointed" or "ordained" elders in each church, as if by autocratic decree from above. In fact, Paul and Barnabas had the believers in the new church bodies nominate and elect (*cheirotoneō*, literally "to raise the hand") the elders. This was in keeping with their own bottom-up, nonauthoritarian vision of leadership.

What we don't find in the New Testament, then, is a model of leadership that is hierarchical, authoritarian, or focused on filling offices. What we do find is a very organic, bottom-up model of leadership. In a church, over time,

certain church members exhibit mature Christian character and come to be known as trustworthy people (1 Tim.
3:2-12; Titus 1:6-9). When they speak, because others
know they are virtuous, truthful people, the body finds
them uncommonly persuasive and readily trusts them.

When these people become known as caring for the
well-being of the church as a whole, they should be recognized and appreciated as people who pastor and oversee
the church (1 Thess. 5:12; Heb. 13:7). Some churches
might formally designate them elders. Others might not.

But whatever authority these leaders have to influence
the church does not reside in formal office nor ability to
coerce others. Rather, it is given to leaders by believers
around them because of the exemplary, trustworthy character of their lives.

Plural, Nonprofessional Church Leadership

How should this bottom-up, New Testament model of
church leadership shape our contemporary churches?

First, leadership in our churches should be de-
professionalized. This will often mean doing away with
the clergy role, a proposal examined in the previous chapter. Church leaders should not automatically be recruited
and hired from outside, the same way a corporation re-
cruits and hires a chief executive officer. Rather, church
leaders should typically emerge, indigenously and organically, out of the local body of believers.

This also means paring back much of the hierarchy and
bureaucracy characterizing many churches today. The old
efforts to justify biblically an elaborate chain-of-command
structure in the church are weak. There is no firm evidence
allowing distinctions in rank or authority between elders,
overseers, bishops, or, for that matter, popes. On the contrary, the biblical term "bishop" (*episkopoi*) simply indi-

cates the nature of such a person's work—overseeing. Meanwhile "elder" (*presbuteroi*) refers to the maturity of character which helps make a person a leader.

Second, Christians ought to forget the idea that church leaders are to rule, control, or make decisions for the church. Leaders should set good examples for others with their own lives. They should oversee—literally, watch over—the church, attending to the big picture of the church's life. And leaders should offer wise counsel to the body when needed. Beyond this, the entire people of God must take active responsibility for the life and direction of the church.

Third, church leadership should be plural. Unlike many contemporary churches, no New Testament church had only one leader. They had many (Acts 14:23; 20:17; Phil. 1:1; 1 Tim. 5:17; Titus 1:5). Having only one leader is dangerous. It tends to nurture autocratic domination. The biblical model should lead us to recognize and appreciate *all* who function as leaders in the church.

Furthermore, no one leader should dominate the others, as professional pastors often overshadow their staff and volunteer co-workers. Rather, in a spirit of unity and collegiality, each leader should submit to the others and to the whole body (Matt. 20:25-27; Eph. 5:21).

Fourth, if a church does formally recognize leaders with titles such as "elder," "overseer," or "deacon," it ought to remember that those titles are descriptions of how those leaders *function* (elders and overseers give mature oversight and deacons serve). They are *not* formal, objective, self-existent offices that must be filled when vacated.

Finally, on the question of paying leaders, in the last chapter we saw in one New Testament passage Paul recommending that hard-working, effective teachers in Ephesus be rewarded for their work with honoraria (1 Tim. 5:17-18). Paying honoraria for their preparations to those who teach in our churches, when such work is performed in addition to regular jobs, makes sense. But this is a far cry from hiring professional, full-time, Christian leaders.

In churches where all members responsibly contribute spiritual gifts, many of the church's unnecessary programs and bureaucracies are eliminated, and leadership is plural and decentralized, the need for paid church leaders will be minimized. With tasks and responsibilities so widely shared within the body, a church's primary financial resources can better be directed elsewhere.

Neither Male nor Female

For much of church history, the Bible has been misread concerning its view of women's place in the church. It has been understood to teach the subordination of women. Only men, the Bible has been thought to say, can hold authority, leadership, and teaching positions in the church. Women should remain quiet and obedient. The consequence of this mistaken view has been to cripple half of the body of Christ.

In fact, this simplistic misreading of the Bible on women simply reflected the broader misreading of the Bible on church authority and leadership in general. Excluding women from church leadership fits well with a commitment to hierarchy, the clergy-laity dichotomy, and the authority of ecclesiastical offices.

In recent decades, however, a wave of respectable, conservative biblical scholars have restudied the texts and reconsidered the traditional view. They have discovered and convincingly argued that far from teaching the subordination of women, the Bible, rightly understood, teaches the equality and freedom of women. It teaches that God created man and women as equal (Gen. 1:26-27) but sin destroyed that equality, making women subservient to men (Gen. 3:16). The gospel, however, cancels and reverses the work of sin, restoring human relationships to their rightful state (2 Cor. 5:17). The work of Christ in the church breaks down the walls that have divided people throughout history, including the wall of male domination (Gal. 3:28).

This corrected reading of the Bible lets us see things in the Scriptures we had missed. We see, for example, women exercising the ministry of prophesy in Caesarea (Acts 21:8-9) and Corinth (1 Cor. 11:5-6). We also see a number of women in Ephesus and Philippi, including Euodia, Synthyche, and Prisca, who were Paul's "fellow-workers" in ministry (Rom. 16:3; Phil. 4:2-3).

We discover Junias, a woman apostle in Rome, whom Paul called, along with her husband, Andronicus, "outstanding among the apostles" (Rom. 16:7, NIV). We find Phoebe, a woman deacon at the church in Cenchrea (Rom. 16:1-2), as well as the presence of women deacons at the church in Ephesus (1 Tim. 3:11). We observe Mary of Rome engaged in the same kind of work (*kopiao*) as were the elders in Ephesus (Rom. 16:6; 1 Tim. 5:17). We notice that fully one-third of those involved in ministry and mission whom Paul greeted in his letter to the Romans were women (Rom. 16:1-16).

We continue to read with new eyes and see that, in Paul's teaching on marriage, the husband is not the final authority and decision maker. Paul instead teaches mutuality and consensus decision making in marriage (1 Cor. 7:4-5). We discover that the New Testament, carefully read, does not command husbands to exercise authority over their wives and wives to obey their husbands. On the contrary, *mutual submission* emerges as the overarching principle of all Christian relationships, both inside and outside marriage (Eph. 5:21-31).

If we study further, we come to understand that in the

oft-quoted passage of 1 Timothy 2:11, Paul was not establishing the silence of women as a universal principle of church order. That would have contradicted Paul's knowledge and hearty approval of all the women ministers noted above. Instead, Paul was responding to a specific crisis situation in Ephesus. There untrained women were spreading strange doctrines (1 Tim. 5:13) and adorning themselves in ways associated with prostitution and idol worship (1 Tim. 2:9-10).

Because of their freedom in Christ, women in the Ephesian church *were* teaching. But because women were generally uneducated in that culture, most apparently did not know enough to distinguish false teachings from true. Hence they were spreading strange, probably gnostic, doctrines in the house churches (1 Tim. 5:13). From the grave concern Paul expresses in this letter, we see that false teachings threatened to destroy faith in Ephesus (1 Tim. 1:3-7, 10; 4:1-3, 7; 6:3-4, 20-21). Thus, Paul's main preoccupation was to reassert orthodox teachings there.

Fearing that he himself would be delayed in coming to Ephesus (1 Tim. 3:14-15), Paul took the drastic but necessary emergency measure of imposing a temporary ban on teaching by women. The best translation of 2:12 is not "I do not permit" but "I am not presently permitting (*epitrepō*, present tense) women to teach." The emphasis is on the situational, impermanent nature of the prohibition. We should read these verses as Paul's emergency instructions, not his standard church polity. And we should see Paul was reacting against *uneducated* teachers, not *women* teachers; and against *false* doctrine, not doctrine taught by *women*.

Obviously, these few paragraphs only begin to explore the issue. There are many more questions to answer and passages to address (1 Cor. 11:3-16; 14:33-35; Eph. 5:22-24). But this is not the place to go into detail. Many other excellent books and articles have already done so (see Appendix A), clearly demonstrating the biblical basis for the emancipation of women.

Realizing that the Bible teaches the full equality and participation of women in church, some Christian feminists have fought to have women ordained as full-time clergy. This is unfortunate. It does not question the system deeply enough. Simply admitting more women into the male-dominated clergy profession is not the answer. Adopting a new model of ministry for both men and women is the answer.

Excluding women from church leadership fits well with a commitment to hierarchy, the clergy-laity distinction, and the authority of ecclesiastical offices. In contrast, the free, full participation of women in church life fits well with emphasis on the spiritual gifts of all people and on organic, decentralized leadership.

When the clerical caste is abolished, whether or not women can belong to it is irrelevant. When leaders organically emerge from a congregation because of their mature Christian character, excluding women makes no sense. When people share gifts of teaching or mercy, whether they are men or women is beside the point. What matters is that *all* contribute gifts for the good of the whole.

Consensus Decision Making

All groups, including churches, have to make decisions. That is good. Decision making is an opportunity to increase communication, unity, and a sense of purpose in a church. But it can also generate turmoil, resentment, and discord. Either outcome largely depends on how decision-making is approached.

Many churches are organized bureaucratically. Hierarchy, management, officers, and committees each play their functional roles to create smooth organizational operation. Bureaucracy, however, requires directed leadership and fragmented, authoritarian decision making. The pastor decides, the elders decide, the committee decides, the trustees decide. Bureaucracy is necessary for IBM and the Department of Defense. But is it appropriate for the family of God, the community of believers?

Bureaucratic leadership and decision making in the church undermines participation, communication, and common purpose. When small groups make decisions that affect the whole without the consensus of the whole, the seeds of discord are sown. When dominating leaders make decisions and call the flock to follow, the seeds of apathy and immaturity are sown.

The radical church renewal alternative is to make decisions by consensus. Consensus means near unanimity. It is reached when most members of a body agree with a decision, and when the few unable to agree put aside objections and support the decision in good faith.

To make a decision by consensus, a proposal is made. The members of the church then evaluate in their minds and hearts what is best for the church. They seek out the leading of the Spirit. The proposal is discussed. Arguments in favor and opposition are heard. Problems are worked out.

Eventually, we hope, the group reaches a consensus and makes a decision. If not, discussion about the issue is continued until a future time when the issue is taken up again and perhaps resolved. In any case, as a matter of principle, decisions are final only when real consensus is reached by the group, when all can say, even if with varying degrees of enthusiasm, "Yes, we will do this."

With consensus, the thoughts and feelings of each person are heard and respected. Consensus draws all church members into the decision-making process. It demands their attention and participation. It requires that they seriously think and pray about issues and work out any differences together.

Consensus makes people own their decisions. Because people actually participate in making decisions, they know the decisions are their responsibility to support and implement. Consensus also tends to eliminate grumbling and complaints about decisions, for in the process no voice is ignored or excluded. With consensus, peoples' problems are expressed and worked out *before* the decision is made. Once consensus is reached, grounds for resistance and opposition have been minimized.

Consensus is built on the experience of Christian community. It requires strong relationships able to tolerate struggling through issues together. It requires mutual love and respect to hear each other when there is disagreement. Consensus also requires a commitment to know and understand other people more than a desire to convince or railroad them.

Consensus, as a way to make decisions in the church, is not easier, just better. To paraphrase Winston Churchill, consensus is the worst form of decision making in the church, except for all the others. Consensus is not strong on efficiency, if by that we mean ease and speed. It can take a long time to work through issues, which can become quite frustrating. While most decisions in my community, for example, are made easily, one of the hardest decisions we faced took us four years to decide.

On the other hand, consensus *is* strong on unity, communication, openness to the Spirit's leading, and responsible participation in the body. In achieving those values, consensus *is* efficient. Deciding by consensus, then, simply requires belief that unity, love, communication, and participation are more important in the Christian scheme of things than quick, easy decisions. It requires the understanding that, ultimately, the process is as important as the outcome. How we treat each other as we make decisions together is as important as what we actually decide.

Pope John Paul II once asserted that the church is not a democracy. He was right. Periodic elections to represent changing interests is hardly the way to run a church. But it is just as true that churches are not hierarchies or bureaucracies. Rather, churches are—or should be—communities of fellowship, households of love, extended families of faith. Making decisions in a way that confirms this reality requires putting decision making in the hands and hearts of all members of a congregation. It requires that we work together, in unity and love, to reach consensus.

How to Grow: Addition or Multiplication?

Doing consensus decision making brings one more important issue into focus: size. It is hard to reach consensus in very large churches. There are too many voices to be heard. Too many divergent views are expressed. There may not enough opportunities to build the trusting, personal relationships which are the basis for working out differences.

Radical church renewal views the size issue as an opportunity, not a problem. The opportunity is to realize that there are alternative ways to handle church growth that better facilitate community, participatory ministry, and decentralized leadership.

The standard method for dealing with church growth is through *addition*. Add more members and add more additions to the church building. Eventually, build a new building. Become one big church. If you really succeed, become a megachurch.

The alternative method for dealing with church growth is through *multiplication*. As you grow, multiply the number of small, interconnected church bodies. Become a closely bound network of smaller churches.

In contemporary culture, bigger is better. But bigger may not be better in the body of Christ. Bigger is more impersonal and inflexible. Bigger needs more regulation and control. Bigger requires more resources simply to be maintained. We would do well to explore better ways to keep churches small, even when we grow.

My church is a network of small house churches. As the house churches grow, they spin off new house churches. In this way, we can grow almost indefinitely without losing our experience of community, ability to do without clergy, decentralized leadership structure, and consensus decision making. At the same time, because we are closely linked, we are also a large group and can enjoy many strengths and benefits of big churches.

Most churches in fact have both large and small groups. But the typical church uses its small groups—Bible studies, prayer meetings, discipleship groups—to manage the inadequacies of the large group, which is considered primary. The alternative is to use a large group—the network— to manage the inadequacies of small groups, which are primary. This alternative structure better retains the beauty of the small, while enjoying the advantages of the large.

This is but a glance at the issue of size in radical church renewal. We will return to the discussion in chapter five.

4

Open Up Worship Services

MANY CHRISTIANS agree that worship is an area of church life that cries out for renewal. The question is, what form should that renewal take? Each church and tradition needs to answer this question for itself. But going to the root calls us to address a number of important considerations having to do with the *structure* of worship.

Structurally, the worship services of many churches are preplanned, clergy-centered, and performance-oriented. Such characteristics profoundly shape our experience of worship and often undermine our best intentions. Radical church renewal asks us to reconsider the whole affair.

Putting Worship into Perspective

The worship of God by believers is not extensively addressed in the New Testament. But some important passages do speak about worship and offer a set of principles that can guide our renewal of worship.

Before we proceed, however, we must note two general points about worship that are not often recognized. First, the primary reason for believers gathering together regularly is not only to worship. Though churches often call their meetings "worship services," the New Testament does not see worship as the only reason for doing church.

In the most extended New Testament teaching on church gatherings (1 Cor. 11:2—14:40), Paul repeatedly states that the overarching goal of meeting together is mutual edification (*oikodomeō*). Edification entails building up and strengthening the believing community.

Paul chastises the Corinthians because their "meetings do more harm than good" (11:17, NIV). He then explains that the gifts of the Spirit are given to each "for the common good" (12:7ff., NIV). Spiritual gifts, Paul argues, should be exercised for people's "*edification*, encouragement, and comfort" (14:3, author's paraphrase), "so that the church may be *edified*" (14:5, NIV). Paul encourages the Corinthians to "try to excel in gifts that *edify* the church" (14:12, author's paraphrase). He discourages gifts that, when exercised, "give thanks well enough, but the other person is not *edified*" (14:17, author's paraphrase). Believers, says Paul, should order their meetings "so that everyone may be instructed and *edified*" (14:31, author's paraphrase). Paul summarizes his argument,

> What then shall we say, brothers? When you come together, everyone has a hymn, or a word of instruction, a revelation, a tongue or an interpretation. *All of these must be done for the edification of the church.* (1 Cor. 14:26, author's paraphrase; also see 12:7-11; emphasis added here, above, and below)

This was not Paul's teaching only to the Corinthians. Paul also wrote to the Christians in Ephesus that the gifts of the Spirit are given to the body "to prepare God's people for works of service, so that the body of Christ may be *edified"* (Eph. 4:12, author's paraphrase). To the believers in Rome, he wrote, "Let us therefore make every effort to do what leads to peace and to *mutual edification"* (Rom. 14:19, NIV).

Second, according to the New Testament, worship is a holistic experience. Worship is not primarily something we do on Sunday mornings but an activity that involves our whole lives. Paul wrote,

> I urge you, brothers, in view of God's mercy, to offer your bodies as living sacrifices, holy and pleasing to God—this is your reasonable act of worship. Do not conform any longer to the pattern of this world, but be transformed by the renewing of your mind. Then you will be able to test and approve what God's will is—his good, pleasing, and perfect will. (Rom. 12:1-2, author's paraphrase; also see 1 Pet. 2:5)

Christians don't worship God in a limited time or place. We worship God with our entire lives and our bodies, by living in obedience to God, not the world. This involves living in love and building up the church (Rom. 12:3-21).

The author of Hebrews writes, "Therefore, since we are receiving a kingdom that cannot be shaken, let us be thankful, and so worship God acceptably with reverence and awe" (Heb. 12:28, NIV). The root meaning of this Greek verb "to worship" (*latreuō*), is *to serve*. We worship God by serving God in the kingdom with our entire lives.

More fundamentally than singing hymns in church, the love, spiritual knowledge and insight, and righteousness of our lives together glorifies and praises God (Phil. 1:11). Thus we offer sacrifices which please God not only by singing, though this has its own place and power. We offer sacrifices also by doing good and sharing with others, "for with such sacrifices God is pleased" (Heb. 13:15-16, NIV).

Of course, worship *itself* is edifying. It has an important place in the community of believers. And while worship finally is expressed in the whole of our lives, we are also to praise God in our meetings together. Thus we return to our initial question: what principles from the New Testament can guide our renewal of community worship?

New Testament Principles of Worship

The first principle is that communal worship is *God-centered*. God alone should be the focus of our minds and hearts as we worship together. Ungodly people worship created things (Rom. 1:25), idols (Acts 7:39-43), wealth (Matt. 6:24), demons (Rev. 9:20), the beast and the dragon (Rev. 13:4, 8, 12, 15; 14:9, 11; 16:2). But Christians worship God alone (Matt. 4:10).

God should be the center around which all worship revolves. Revelation 4 conveys a powerful vision of heavenly worship in which God sits on a throne surrounded by twenty-four elders and four living creatures (4:2-7). The four living creatures continually proclaim God's holiness (4:8), while the elders fall before the throne and lay down their crowns, heralding God's worthiness to receive glory and honor and power (4:10-11). This majestic vision is our model. God is fully the center and focus of worship.

Second, worship is *collective*, an exercise of the body. The wishes of Lone Ranger Christians notwithstanding, worship is primarily a communal activity of the people of God, of the entire congregation of believers. Peter says,

> You are a chosen people, a royal priesthood, a holy nation, a people belonging to God, that you may declare the praises of him who called you out of darkness into his wonderful light. Once you were not a people, but now you are the people of God. (1 Pet. 2:9-10, NIV)

Believers worship God as communities, having "come together" (1 Cor. 14:26) with "one another" (Eph. 5:19;

Col. 3:16). And the pronouns of worship are primarily collective, not individual. *We* offer *our* praise for what God
has done for *us*—not *I* offer *mine* for *me* (e.g., Eph. 1:3-14;
Heb. 12:28). Individually each of us is only one stone that,
to become God's temple, needs to be built into a common
spiritual house so we can offer spiritual sacrifices to God
(1 Pet. 2:5). So collective is the nature of worship that, in
the end, entire nations will worship God (Rev. 15:4).

A third and related point is that worship is *participatory.*
Worship is not a spectator sport. It requires the active involvement and contribution of each believer (1 Cor. 14:26;
Eph. 5:18-19). Each Christian must contribute a gift as a
priest before God offering spiritual sacrifices.

Fourth, worship is *physically active.* The worship of God
is not passive or stationary. It involves our bodies in motion. The Hebrew word for worship (*shakhah*) means "to
bow down" or "to prostrate oneself." Interestingly, the
Greek word for worship most commonly used in the Bible
(*proskuneō*) means literally "to kiss toward" (from *pros*, "toward," and *kuneō*, "to kiss"). Anyone who has gotten down
to the ground on knees or face or really kissed another
person knows these are corporeal, active operations. They
involve bodies. They require physical motion.

The worshiping elders in heaven bowed to the ground
before God (Rev. 4:10-11), as did Isaac (Gen. 24:48), Moses (Exod. 34:8), the Israelites (2 Chron. 29:28, 30), Daniel
(Dan. 10:15), the magi (Matt. 2:11). Every human that has
lived will bow (Rom. 14:11; Phil. 2:10). David, with shouts
and trumpets, "danced before the Lord with all his might"
(2 Sam. 6:14, NIV; 1 Chron. 15:28-29). And God promises
that upon the redemption of God's people they will dance
before God with joy (Jer. 31:4,13). The psalmist says "Lift
up your hands in the sanctuary and praise the Lord" (Ps.
134:2, NIV). Paul declares, "I want every person everywhere to lift up holy hands in prayer" (1 Tim. 2:8, author's
paraphrase).

Some churches may not believe in physically active worship. They may say that the ideas of bowing and kissing only symbolize an inward attitude of reverence, honor, adoration, and love. They do symbolize these. But there is no reason why worship must consist only of a subjective attitude in our hearts (although different levels of comfort with body involvement in worship deserve respect).

Fifth, worship is not a merely human activity, but a *Spirit-led* activity. It is the Spirit of God that gives us spiritual gifts (1 Cor. 12, 14) and the Holy Spirit through whom we worship (Phil. 3:3). Jesus told the Samaritan woman,

> A time is coming and has now come when the true worshipers will worship the Father in spirit and truth, for they are the kind of worshipers the Father seeks. God is a Spirit and his worshipers must worship in spirit and in truth. (John 4:23-24, NIV)

Notice the close connection Paul makes between our worship and the Holy Spirit in us.

> Do not get drunk on wine, which leads to debauchery. Instead, be filled with the Spirit. Speak to one another with psalms, hymns and spiritual songs. Sing and make music in your heart to the Lord. (Eph. 5:18-19, NIV)

In warning the Philippian believers against the Judaizers, Paul boasts, "It is . . . we who worship by the Spirit of God, who glory in Christ Jesus" (Phil. 3:3, NIV). The Holy Spirit must lead and empower our worship.

Finally, worship is *narrative*. It tells stories. In fact, the Greek word for praise (*aineō*) also means "to tell" or "to narrate." Standing in a long biblical tradition, we worship by narrating the great things God has done in history and in our lives. The mighty deeds of God were the source, for example, of the worship of the psalmist.

My mouth is filled with your praise, declaring your splen-
dor all day long. . . . My mouth will tell of your righteousness, of your salvation. . . . I will come and proclaim your
mighty acts, O Sovereign Lord; I will proclaim your righteousness, yours alone. Since my youth, O God, you have
taught me, and to this day I declare your marvelous deeds.
. . . Do not forsake me, O God, till I declare your power to
the next generation, your might to all who are to come. (Ps.
71:8, 15-18, NIV)

Likewise, Paul praised God by telling the great story of
God's redemptive work. Paul told of how God blessed us,
chose us, predestined us, adopted us, redeemed us, gave
Jesus to us, forgave us, and gave us wisdom and understanding (Eph. 1:3-14). God did all this "to the praise of his
glorious grace" (1:6, NIV) and "to the praise of his glory"
(1:14, NIV).

Similarly, throughout the Bible, God is praised for
works of mercy, salvation, and healing (e.g., Exod. 15:1-21;
1 Chron. 16:7-36; Dan. 3:28-29; Luke 2:13-14, 20; 18:43;
19:37; Acts 3:8-9).

Pews, Pulpits, and Programs

In theory at least, most churches endorse the above
principles. Unfortunately, the actual structures of many
worship services often obstruct putting these principles
into practice. Churches thus often talk one reality and live
another.

Three church "p's"—pews, pulpits, and programs—
present the biggest structural obstacles to biblical worship.

The word "pew" is an Old French derivative (*pui*) of the
Latin word *podium*, which means, tellingly, "a balcony."
Pews came into existence in European churches sometime
after 1450, replacing three-legged stools. For centuries af-

ter, church pews were leased or owned and could be bequeathed in a will.

Pews, usually separated into compartments with low walls, often established a hierarchy in churches. They were usually allotted to families and institutions according to social rank. Owners or renters of pews could and did sue those who trespassed on or disturbed their pew space.

Pews, true to their etymological origin, are essentially balconies, detached seatings from which to watch performances. Pews are immobile, inflexible, regimenting structures that divide congregations—like bottles on the store shelf—into neatly ordered lines all facing in the same direction. Pews atomize and demobilize congregations. They thwart the New Testament principles that worship should be collective and physically active.

A church, for example, may *wish* to foster a collective, community spirit in worship, so that members worship God as *a people*, not just a collection of individuals. But these same churches then seat everyone in straight rows of hard pews permanently screwed to the floor. In this setup, the only thing people can see, besides the minister at the pulpit, are the backs of other people's heads!

As Howard Snyder, in his groundbreaking book, *The Problem of Wineskins*, wrote, "It is as if the ideal was to put each worshiper in his own private isolation booth so he could see only the minister and not be distracted by other people." Pews ensure almost no human interaction, touching, or eye contact during the church meeting. If the face of the whole body of Christ is radiant with joy or filled with tears, people in pews have a hard time knowing it. This defeats a communal sense of worship.

Similarly, a church may want to open itself up to more physically expressive motion in worship. But the rigidity and immobility of pews get in the way. It's hard enough to sway, kneel, or hug the person in front of you with pews.

Imagine trying to dance in worship together through pews. Consequently, in many churches with pews, the main movement of the congregation is parents leaning over to tell children to sit still.

Pews do more than provide seating for churchgoers. Pews create a subtly regimented atmosphere and separate people from each other, making community and active worship unnecessarily difficult. Some experimental, progressive churches now have cinema-style seats, but the outcome is nearly the same.

Pulpits also obstruct worship according to New Testament principles. Pulpits came into churches in the thirteenth century. They replaced reading tables, called *ambos,* from which, for previous centuries, the Gospels and epistles were read.

Originally *ambos* were simply portable lecterns. But by the sixth century, they became fixed church furnishings. Seven centuries later, they were replaced by pulpits. The word "pulpit" comes from the Latin word *pulpitum,* which means, again tellingly, "a stage."

Pulpits *are* stages. They are platforms before audiences from which worship services are orchestrated and even performed. Pulpits elevate clergy, physically and symbolically, to positions of prominence and authority. They focus congregational attention on one person, the minister, inevitably and intentionally making him or her central.

But New Testament worship has little use for stages or performances. In a pulpit-focused church, worship again tends to become a spectator sport. God-centered and participatory worship is obstructed. It is the minister on whom all eyes focus. It is the minister at the pulpit who does almost all the talking. The congregation gets to sing occasionally, but only when someone in the pulpit says so. Even then, the congregation only sings the song and verses or recites the readings as directed. While this activity is commonly known as "leading" worship, it can degenerate into "dictating" worship.

Churches may sincerely want their worship to be centered on God. But by focusing the congregation's attention on the pulpit and the minister, they may defeat that desire. Churches may likewise want worship to be participatory and narrative. But by having the minister direct and dominate almost the entire meeting from "the stage," they again make meeting their goal more difficult.

The third obstacle in Christian worship is the pre-planned program. Most churches have preestablished programs, called the "order of worship," for their meetings. These are often typed and printed in bulletins which are handed out to members as they enter the sanctuary. The service consists of proceeding through this list of events, as directed by the minister.

Why construct preestablished programs to lock in the order of our worship? What does that accomplish? Unlike the church in Corinth (1 Cor. 14:22-40), it's not as if most established churches are so bordering on chaos that they need to be regulated and contained. Typically, the problem with traditional churches is the opposite.

Certainly many worship services which follow a pre-established order are dynamic and spirit-filled. A valid case can be made for such worship styles, which deserve respect even from those of us who do not prefer them.

Yet uncritical use of closed-ended, preestablished programs often hinders open-ended, Spirit-led, participatory worship. All believers are priests before God, called to contribute their special gifts in worship (1 Cor. 14:26-27; Eph. 5:19; 1 Pet. 2:9). Thus, according the vision of radical church renewal, it should be possible in church for believers to participate in countless ways. This can include giving thanksgivings and testimonies, confessing sins, reading from the Bible, audibly praising God, sharing difficulties and lessons learned, interceding in prayer, meditating together, and encouraging or challenging each other.

Many churches fail to put New Testament principles of worship into practice. This is usually not because of the beliefs or intentions of the Christians involved, but because of the structures and patterned routines of churches, such as pews, pulpits, and programs. Renewing worship, then, means changing church structures and routines.

Structural Changes

In the end, each church and tradition must determine for itself exactly what changes will renew worship according to New Testament principles. The changes necessary in a Pentecostal church, for example, will not be identical to those in an Episcopal church. Still, similar transformations will probably be necessary among many types of churches. What follows is one proposal for such changes.

First, churches should tear out all pews and pulpits. In place of the pews, churches should buy padded folding chairs and set them up in concentric circles with aisles, so participants face each other. Folding chairs are flexible and mobile. They can be set up and moved around as needed. They also can be stored easily when room is needed for other activities.

Second, churches should have facilitators, not worship leaders/directors. Instead of having the same person lead the service week after week from the front (in a circle there is no front), various members should take turns as meeting facilitators.

Facilitators sit *with* the congregation. Their role is not to direct everything that happens in worship. It is to keep an eye on time and to facilitate transitions when needed. They might say, for example, "Perhaps now we should spend some time in prayer," "Now Joe has a teaching to share with us today," or "It's almost time to end. Are there announcements?" Unlike the minister as worship leader, the worship facilitator's role is provisional, unobtrusive, and nonauthoritarian.

Third, churches should let flexibility, not rigid pre-planning, be their guide. Churches oriented toward radical renewal should abandon or pare back preplanned programs of worship. Churches should not determine only ahead of time, with paper and ink, exactly what will transpire during meetings. They should leave meetings flexible and open-ended. This does not mean services will be chaotic and formless, however. Churches will develop their own informal orders of worship, even when flexible. Furthermore, facilitators help give order and form to meetings. The goal is elimination not of order but rigidity.

Such changes inspire a worship atmosphere which invites the appropriate participation of all. The structure and tone of worship ought to encourage members to share testimonies, insights, fears, prayer requests, confessions, Scripture passages, and song requests. The schedule of teaching and preaching should be opened to whoever has such gifts.

Other changes could also be helpful. Churches might spend time discussing the meaning and practical applications of teachings immediately following input, either in small groups or together. Through these discussions, questions can be asked, miscommunications clarified, new insights added, and the teaching's practical implications further explored. There is no necessity or benefit from having sermons be only one-way communications. In fact, the word sermon comes from the Latin *sermo*, which actually means "a dialogue"!

Churches could change the language of songs and readings, replacing individualistic pronouns (I, me, my) with collective pronouns (we, us, our). While we're at it, we ought to replace our centuries-old, King James "thees" and "thous" with their contemporary equivalents.

Churches should also cultivate an atmosphere where it is acceptable to let our hair down and physically express worship of God. Christians might take a hint from African American gospel choirs and let bodies sway with the rhythms of songs. Believers might take a hint from charismatics and lift hands to God in praise. Worshipers might take a hint from high liturgy and get down on their knees in reverence. Worshipers might learn to tap their feet, to clap, to hold hands, maybe even to dance together.

Churches can experiment with other new ideas. Try learning and writing some new Scripture songs, hymns, or choruses. Try introducing new accompanying instruments—such as guitars, percussion instruments, recorders—in worship. Instead of a didactic teaching, try presenting a drama skit now and then for the congregation to reflect on or discuss. Occasionally try orienting the activities of the entire church meeting around the children of the congregation. On a nice day, try holding the meeting outdoors in a local park.

Church renewal that makes a difference catches a vision of worship that is communal, open, participatory, Spirit-led, God-centered. The worship service, if judged at all, is evaluated not by the oratorical brilliance of the sermon or goosebump-raising performance of the choir, but by the deepening faith of the saints and the glorification of God.

Our Dressed-Up Selves

One more common worship practice deserves further consideration. Most North American Christians dress up for church. That can be a problem. "Come on," someone might say. "Whether or not we get dressed up for church is hardly a burning issue—certainly not a key issue of church renewal." Fair enough. No use making a mountain out of a molehill over dressy church clothes. But it's not the clothes that are the problem. It's what the nice clothes represent.

Dressing only in our best on Sunday morning is not a big deal. But it is symptomatic of a problem that is a big deal. People bring to church too often only their nice selves, attractive selves, dressed-up selves. Leaving our real selves, the selves our families see, at home and bringing only our dressy selves to church risks turning church into two hours of "impression management."

When you look at church in terms of presentation of self and impression management, you see a frightening resemblance with stage show business. All the elements are there: costumes, a master of ceremonies, makeup, a script, a stage, ushers, music, a chorus, an audience, props, lighting, and programs. The only differences are occasional audience participation and the lack of tickets and popcorn!

But church is not a show. Church is not a place for actors and actresses. Church is community. We shouldn't have to dress up for each other, either literally or figuratively. We should leave impression management at our jobs. At church we should be at home. Church should be a place where our authentic selves, feeling accepted, can relax.

I'm not arguing that Sunday morning should become a kind of ecclesiastical Roller Derby or primal scream therapy session. There is a place for common civility. There is a place for careful dressing. But civility has limits. Careful dressing can become preening; it can make us compete to see who can wear the finest, most expensive outfits. When civility or competitive dressing become the dominant tones of our fellowship, church itself turns inauthentic and superficial. And nobody wants a superficial church.

Part of the problem is that again for many church amounts only to few hours on Sunday morning. Sometimes our authentic selves are not nice. That's okay. Yet if our lives aren't intertwined in community where we share our real selves during the week, if two hours a week is all we have with other believers, we will never have the nerve to bring our authentic selves to Sunday morning. We will only bring our best-dressed selves.

One rotten fruit of a church whose members preen is the inflated illusion of the collective righteousness of the congregation. People know how sinful and weird they themselves are. But they never admit it in a church which pressures them to look good, be nice, and come across like every other good Christian.

Consequently, people never see that everyone else is as strange and messed up as they are. They pretend to be better than they are and simultaneously often feel guilty because they don't live up to their own act. And they certainly don't live up to the (illusory) righteousness of others.

That dehumanizes us. It's also a false witness to the world. We aren't in church because we're good. We're there because we're rotten but have asked God to forgive us. If we feign righteousness with each other, we tell the world church is a place for good people (translate: hypocrites). "So it's not a place for me." We communicate an anti-gospel of works-righteousness.

The Bible tells us to confess our sins to one another (James 5:16). This may mean various things, but it can't mean presenting only polished selves to each other. Radical church renewal calls us to make church a place of family and authenticity instead of performance. It bids us relax, let our hair down, take the focus off how nice we look (and how good we are). It calls us instead to see the wonderful works God has done and is doing among us.

5

Overcome the Edifice Complex

A FRIEND of mine belongs to a young, growing church in an affluent suburb. They meet in a rented hall. But they want to build their own building. The problem is they don't have the money. The engineering costs simply for designing the building and preparing the work site will be $160,000. But, this friend wrote in a letter, they are not worried. They believe God wants them to get a building, so they are trusting God for the money.

As I read his letter, I couldn't help wondering whether God really wanted another church building built at a cost of $160,000 just for starters.

The Bible calls God's people pilgrims, sojourners, and strangers in this unbelieving world. Our hope and faith, safety and sustenance are to be found in God alone. Our roots are to be sunk only in God's kingdom.

Like Abraham, we are called to an alert readiness to drop everything, if need be, and go where God leads. Or, as Vernard Eller writes in his provocative book, *The Out-*

ward Bound, the church is called to be a caravan, a group of people banded together to seek a common destination. We are not to be a commissary, an institution commissioned to dispense goods and services to a select constituency. Like the Samaritan woman, God's people are called to worship God, not on a mountain or in the temple, but in spirit and truth.

But the way many churches today are organized betrays a comfortably entrenched immobility and inflexibility. Few contemporary churches conjure up images of sojourners or pilgrims. The more likely image is of a well-established, comfortable corporation, or voluntary association.

Perhaps the most obvious monument to the church's immobility and inflexibility are its church buildings. Buildings don't move, they are designed *not* to move. Buildings are massive, stationary structures, imposing physical symbols of fixity and rigidity. For these and other reasons, Howard Snyder has rightly argued that church buildings witness to the immobility, inflexibility, lack of fellowship, pride, and class divisions of the modern church.

Christians throughout the centuries have tended toward love affairs with edifices. They have fancied temple over tabernacle, cathedral over caravan, palace over pilgrimage. Today we are stricken with this edifice complex more than ever. Scarcely does a new congregation get started before it starts thinking about securing its own building—as if the brick and glass somehow make it more legitimately a church.

Going to the root challenges us to reconsider how we think about our church buildings. It calls us to reexamine our priorities and begin to explore more dynamic, flexible forms of organization and structure that better symbolize and facilitate adaptability, humility, creativity, and good stewardship.

No Place Like Home

If you could ask a Christian in the first church, "Where is your church located?" the answer would probably be a puzzled look. For the first two hundred years of church history—ten generations of Christians—there were no church buildings that could have had locations. The church (*ekklēsia*) then was not understood as a building or even an organization. It was the gathered community of people who believed in Jesus.

But, without church buildings, where did these believers gather? In the most natural place for any family—in this case, the family of God—to gather: their homes.

That the homes of believers were the centers of activity for the first Christians is clear in the New Testament. Between Jesus' ascension and Pentecost, the apostles met to pray in a home (Acts 1:14, 2:2). After Pentecost, the first believers broke bread in their homes (Acts 2:46). When Saul or the Jews set out to persecute groups of Christians, they looked for Christians meeting in houses (Acts 8:3; 17:5). After Peter was miraculously freed from prison by an angel, he went straight to Mary's house where many believers were gathered to pray (Acts 12:12).

The churches in Philippi and Corinth were begun in homes when entire households were converted and baptized (Acts 16:11-15, 31-34; 18:7-8; 1 Cor. 1:16). Paul preached the gospel not only in the temple courts, but from home to home (Acts 5:42; 20:20; also see 2 John 10). After Paul and Silas were freed from the Philippian jail, they went to Lydia's house where they met with and encouraged new believers (Acts 16:40). The churches in Rome, Colosse, and Ephesus met in believers' houses (Rom. 16:5, 23; 1 Cor. 16:19; Col. 4:15; Philem. 2; 1 Tim. 5:13; 2 Tim. 3:6).

These early Christians *could* have followed the familiar model of the Jewish temple or synagogue and created specifically Christian buildings to meet and worship in. They did not. Apparently they believed their homes were the best context for gathering. Of course, the persecution they faced may have encouraged this practice, so we need to be cautious about drawing simplistic conclusions.

Whatever factors made early Christians gather in homes, the practice makes sense. Homes are a place of family, which is what early believers were to each other (Gal. 6:10; Heb. 2:11). Homes are where children belong —notice that children participated in the first churches (Eph 6:1-3; Col. 3:20). Homes are natural places for hospitality (Rom. 12:13; 1 Pet. 4:9) and for eating together— early Christians celebrated the Lord's Supper by eating, not a wafer or bit of bread, but an entire meal together (e.g., 1 Cor. 11:17-34). And because home is the context in which everyday life is lived, homes provide natural settings for the building of ongoing relationships of community and fellowship among the people of God. A home is a center of life; a church building is just a place to meet.

The Church Comes Home

For these and other reasons, hundreds of thousands of Christians all over the world are leaving church buildings. They are returning to the home as the place for Christian gatherings. There are home church movements in North America, England, Italy, Australia, China, the Netherlands, Germany, India, East Africa, and most Latin American countries.

The Latin American church, for example, has witnessed an explosion of what are called base ecclesial communities (BECs). BECs are small (typically twenty to forty-five members), neighborhood-based churches which meet in homes or community buildings. They usually are lay-led and emphasize participation, community, and social activism. In a typical BEC meeting, the members discuss personal and community problems, study the Bible, sing, pray, fellowship, and possibly celebrate the eucharist or plan a future ministry or activity.

BECs are helping Latin America Christians take responsibility for their lives, church, and societies in ways the large, institutional church could and did not. In the last thirty years, the number of BECs in Latin America has grown from zero to over two hundred thousand.

Across the South Pacific from Latin America, a band of Christians in Canberra, Australia, meet in a network of house churches, the down-under equivalent of a Latin American BEC. On a weekend evening, several families and singles, about twenty in all, gather at a member's house (the meetings are rotated each month among the various homes). Each contributes to a dinner, which they share together in memory of Jesus' death and resurrection.

The children are members too. They participate as much as they want to and can. After dinner some in the group clean up while others do a Bible lesson with the children. Then the whole group moves to the living room to talk, read Scripture, hear and discuss a short teaching, sing, and pray for each other. When the children get sleepy, their parents put them down in a nearby bedroom until the meeting is over.

Sometimes the meeting is fun and lighthearted; sometimes the group deals with very personal and serious matters. Four or five hours later, the drowsy members gather their children and belongings and head home. During the week, members of the house church will get together for various activities. Every six weeks all the home churches in the city meet together in a rented hall or a park for a worship celebration or social event.

On the other side of the Indian Ocean from the Australians, home churches are popping up all over East Africa.

When the weather is nice, neighborhood Christians gather in a yard, sit on the ground, and do hand work while they sing and hear a Bible teaching. The openness, fellowship, and community of their home churches suit their traditional tribal heritage better than dressing up to sit in wooden pews and sing European hymns in a big, neocolonial church.

Where Your Treasure Is

We might question church buildings, not only because there is no biblical justification for them, and not only because homes are more naturally suited for family-of-God gatherings. The biblical call to good stewardship of our wealth also compels us to reconsider our attitudes about church buildings.

North American Christians have great wealth, a portion of which is spent on church buildings. Conservative estimates place the value of real estate owned by churches in the United States today at over two hundred and thirty-two billion dollars or $232,965,150,000. [This figure is based on these facts and conservative estimates: The market value of church real estate in 1968 was $79.5 billion (M. Yinger, *The Scientific Study of Religion*, 1970). The value of new church construction between 1968-84 was $20.819 billion (*Statistical Abstract*, 1986; *U.S. Department of Commerce, Bureau of Census, Construction Reports 1979-84; Handbook of American and Canadian Churches*, 1980). Estimating the average annual rate of appreciation of church properties at 4 percent between 1968 and 1990. The properties are sold at a 25 percent loss in value due to market glut. Church building debt service and maintenance consumes about 18 percent of the $11,672,316,000 tithed to churches annually (*Statistical Abstract*, 1986.)]

Furthermore, Christians spend additional millions annually for the heating, cooling, and maintenance of these buildings. If all church buildings were sold, another $2.1 billion would be easily saved annually—through money not spent on debt service and maintenance.

Is this good stewardship? How else might we spend God's money? Imagine, if you can, all the churches in the United States making the radical decision to sell their church properties over the next ten years (to be converted to other non-church uses).

Picture all these congregations then either meeting in large, rented public buildings or forming themselves into house churches which would meet together in rented public buildings every few weeks. Then imagine these churches investing all the money from the sale of their church buildings into trust funds and each year spending the earned interest (let us say 9 percent) on missions and ministry. What could churches to do with that money?

Suppose Christians spent only the interest earned on the invested money (not taking into account money not spent on debt service and maintenance, which could also go into service projects). We could comfortably do the following every year, year after year:

- Support translators to translate the Bible into the three thousand languages and dialects presently without a Bible translation ($135 million)
- Feed five million starving or malnourished people every day ($1.82 billion)
- Start and fund seventy-five Christian colleges and theology schools in eastern Europe and Russia ($375 million)
- Support three hundred Christian candidates running for office in the Senate and House of Representatives who would work for consistent pro-life ethic policies ($150 million)

- Send one hundred thousand "tent-maker" missionaries to China to teach English and spread the gospel to
  their Communist students ($250 million)
- Send six hundred thousand underprivileged children
  to Christian summer camp ($180 million)
- Finance new water and sewer systems in one hundred
  thousand Third World villages, eliminating the cause of
  many deadly diseases ($100 million)
- Finance fifteen hundred counseling centers to provide
  low-cost Christian counseling to families and
  individuals in trouble ($600 million)
- Print and ship to Hong Kong one small library of basic
  Christian books for each of the forty thousand under
  ground house churches in China, to be smuggled in by
  "tent-making" missionaries over time ($15 million)
- Fund a Christian environmentalist political lobby to
  work for the proper care of God's natural creation in
  government policy ($80 million)
- Supplement the incomes of five thousand needy re-
  tired ministers ($50 million)
- Build, staff, and supply fifty thousand Christian
  elementary schools in Africa, Asia, and Latin America
  ($700 million)
- Supplement the incomes of one quarter of the 5.2
  million handicapped and elderly Americans who live
  below the poverty line to raise them out of poverty ($4
  billion)
- Support seventy thousand church-planting missionaries to unreached peoples to plant and nourish indige-
  nous churches, almost doubling the number of missionaries on the field today ($1.5 billion)
- Offer $10,000 a year of child support assistance to
  every teenager who is considering having an abortion
  because of lack of financial support, assuming 25 percent accept it ($1.0875 billion)

- Supplement basic medical supplies to eighty thousand Third World hospitals and clinics ($350 million)
- Give financial aid to cut the tuition of eight thousand Christian college students in half ($56 million)
- Finance ten thousand Christian leadership training centers in the Third World ($400 million)
- Set up an interest-free, revolving loan fund to help one hundred thousand Christians every five years finance solar heating, insulation and/or weatherization for their homes ($800 million)
- Support twenty thousand orphanages in Brazil, providing shelter and food for over one million children ($450 million)
- Send ten thousand Third World Christian leaders to Bible college or seminary ($210 million)
- Finance a Christian peace academy to research realistic ways to reduce international military conflicts and the threat of nuclear and chemical war ($800 million)
- Support ten thousand inner city evangelistic and social action ministries ($290 million)
- Finance theological and pastoral training for eight hundred thousand nonprofessional church leaders ($1.3 billion)
- Provide food, clothing, and basic housing for two-thirds of all homeless Americans today ($5 billion)
- Financially help churches in transition from meeting in church buildings to homes and public halls ($267 million)

Yes, But. . . . But What?

But that's impossible! charge skeptics. The churches could never do this! Bunk. In fact, many churches do exactly this. My church, for example, does not spend a dime on a professional pastor or a church building. Consequently, about

95 percent of all our church collections go to missions, evangelism, and ministry to the needy. This is the same annual dollar amount churches twenty times our size spend. We're a small church, but we can do big things with the little money we have because we don't sink it into clergy, mortgages, and maintenance.

Of course, the idea of selling all church buildings and ceasing to build new ones seems incredibly radical. That's because it *is* radical. But it certainly is not impossible. If most churches don't do it, it's not because they can't do it. It's because they won't do it. Radical, yes. But radical might be exactly what the church today needs.

Yes, reply the skeptics, but in the Old Testament, God had the people build a beautiful temple for worship. Doesn't that offer a model to justify contemporary church buildings? Interesting question. But no.

The temple as a place of worship in the old covenant has been replaced by a new kind of temple in the new covenant. With the incarnation, Christ's body became the new temple (John 2:19-21). And as the body of Christ, God's people are God's new temple. "We are the temple of the living God" (2 Cor. 6:16; also see 1 Cor. 3:9, 16-17; 6:19; Eph. 2:20-22; 1 Pet. 2:5).

In the new covenant, the stone building is replaced by the living body. Is it any wonder, then, that in heaven—the ultimate place of worship—there is no temple to be found but the Lord God Almighty and the Lamb (Rev. 21:22)?

Yes, reply the skeptics, but we need buildings for the church to keep growing. How can the church grow without buildings? Well, in all of church history, the period with the greatest rate of church growth (when the gospel spread throughout the known world) was the first two hundred years. This was precisely the time Christians did not have church buildings!

More recently in China, the gospel without church

buildings has spread like wildfire. For decades, many missionaries labored with only moderate success to establish traditional churches in China. When missionaries were expelled from China by the Communists in the 1950s, Chinese Christians began meeting secretly in homes. Since then their home churches have proliferated. Today there are more than forty thousand home churches in China. The number of Protestants has grown from one million in the 1950s to more than forty million today! This despite— or perhaps because of—the absence of church buildings.

Yes, house churches need to be small enough to fit into homes. But that doesn't mean they don't grow. House churches grow simply by multiplying more and more related house churches rather than adding more and more members to the same large church.

Studies indicate that if and when churches do grow, they typically only grow until their buildings are full. Then they stop growing. So church buildings, with all their fixity and inflexibility, often *stop* successful church growth!

Yes, reply the skeptics, but church fellowship halls, kitchens, classrooms, and gyms can be used for outreach ministries and other worthwhile church functions.

That's a reasonable point. At least it is in the case of churches which build church facilities that are functional and use them to their capacity.

But many churches simply build a worship sanctuary with limited functional value and use it only a few hours a week. Think how many church sanctuaries are locked up, cold and empty, about 97 percent of the time.

In addition, church buildings are not the only facilities available for useful activities. All sorts of appropriate, cost-effective recreational, dining, and meeting facilities can be rented for any activity or ministry as needed.

Buildings as Barriers

Even when church facilities lend themselves to outreach ministries, a sizable and important segment of the American population will never step foot into a church building for any reason. I know a number of people like this. A woman who recently joined our community never did, would, or will go into a church building, even after becoming a zealous Christian in her thirties. For her it was house church or nothing. These alienated people have *had* it with the established church and anything associated with it—often with good reason.

Of course, these people would be happy to come to your house for dinner or to the park for a picnic on the weekend. They would welcome involvement in any number of other activities and places that present opportunities for relationships, outreach, and evangelism. But when we insist on building-based outreach, we make church buildings a stumbling block for these people. For many in an increasingly post-Christian culture, our church buildings (which are biblically not essential) get in the way of the kingdom of God. This may not be a trivial problem, since ultimately the only legitimate stumbling-block to the kingdom should be the cross of Christ (1 Cor. 9:19-23; Rom. 14:13; 1 Cor. 1:23; 8:9; 2 Cor. 6:3).

I know a man named Jack in California who understands these alienated people and has started a church for them. Only Jack's church does not call itself church, but "Matthew's Party." And Matthew's Party does not meet in a church building. It meets in a barroom that is otherwise closed on Sundays. With Bible studies, discussions, and prayer, Jack packs out that barroom with baby boomers who have a deep spiritual hunger but would never "go to church." Now that's flexibility for the kingdom. That's creativity in a post-Christian culture.

Vehicles or Burdens?

We live in a world where many people, many Christians, die for lack of rice and beans. We inhabit a post-Christian culture where the usual trappings of the established church are as much a stumbling block as a help to the gospel. We live at a time and place in history full of need and opportunity that our resources could address.

Are we wise, then, to spend so much of our resources on church buildings, mortgages, and maintenance? Or should the need for ministry and mission compel us to become more creative, flexible, and mobile in the way we organize and structure our church lives?

Nice church buildings certainly delight pastors, building committees, congregations. They please the architects and builders who make money designing and building them. But do they glorify the God who traverses the universe yet chooses to meet us and make a home in our hearts? Do they please the God who scorns the high and mighty, lying down among the poor and outcast?

We may love our buildings. But it is far from clear that God does. Indeed, God seems to have abandoned the stone temple model on the day Christ was born.

We may think we can't survive without church buildings. But that's an illusion. We've seen that Christians past and present have survived and thrived without church buildings.

We may enjoy the churchy paraphernalia on which we spend God's money—pulpits, hardwood pews, carpeting, drapery, landscaping, lighting, silver offering plates, choir robes, stained glass. But the Bible says that temple worship is hateful to God when the poor go hungry (Amos 5:7-15, 21-24; Jer. 7:4-7).

We may not have realized there are alternative ways to do church without church buildings. But there are. And these ways are arguably more appropriate for creatively dealing with the post-Christian, fellowship-hungry culture we face today.

I am not saying that God commands Christians to get rid of all church buildings tomorrow. The Bible does not clearly prohibit church buildings. I *am* saying this: If we put together the biblical nonsupport for church buildings, our desperately needy world, the challenges of our post-Christian culture, the opportunities of home-based church, and a little common sense, the burden of proof shifts to those in favor of church buildings.

We must at least challenge our edifice-complex by questioning our love affair with expensive church buildings. Beyond that Christians, in the name of stewardship and creativity, ought seriously to consider stepping out of the safety and familiarity of their church buildings. They might soon discover what so many believers now have. That is that, while traveling on the road to the kingdom, church buildings are not so much convenient vehicles which carry us as enormous burdens we have too long carried.

6

Cultivate a Grace-ful Spirituality of Everyday Life

WHAT DOES radical church renewal say about spirituality? How ought Christian communities committed to going to the root think about relating to God in everyday existence? How should we lean into life as believers living in a crazy world?

Popular Christianity is not short on answers to these questions. Indeed, the airwaves of Christian thought today are cluttered with numerous brands and formulas of spirituality. Many are guilt-inducing, introspective, legalistic, and overly individualistic. Christians of all stripes suffer from these unhealthy spiritualities; nonbelievers of all kinds are justifiably turned off by them.

Radical church renewal calls us to rethink spirituality. It summons us to learn and live a new spirituality of everyday life, one that is steeped in grace. But learning this new spirituality will require unlearning other, more popular varieties of spirituality.

There Are No Formulas with God

The first thing we need to learn is that Christian spirituality is not a matter of finding the right formula. A computer programmer friend of mine once commented with apparent seriousness, "What we need is a formula for creativity." I chuckle over that absurd contradiction. But sometimes I wonder if that's how we treat our life with God.

Have you recently browsed through the average Christian bookstore? What an assortment of programs, plans, guidelines, principles, and formulas to make your life healthy, holy, and happy! There are formulas for Christian dating, powerful preaching, Christian marriage, church growth, even Christian dieting. It's so simple. Just buy the book or tape and follow the plan.

Better yet, save yourself the trouble of leaving the house; just tune into Sunday morning television. Choose your formula for spiritual success simply by changing the station. What will it be this week? Name it and claim it? The be-happy-attitudes? Give to get? Or how about believe and be healed? Whatever your choice, do remember to send the money that keeps your spiritual star on the air.

Formulas are nice. They make life predictable. They guarantee that if we do X, we'll get Y. It's like baking a cake —just follow the recipe and it'll turn out great every time. The only problem is, God does not work by formulas and even seems not to like them. In fact, God makes a habit of debunking them when possible.

Nevertheless, God-in-a-box is what we so often want. Magic is safer than relationship, ritual easier than experience. Indeed, God-in-a-box is what people have always liked. Yet God won't be put in a box. No, God blows boxes apart every time.

Remember Job and his friends? They had it all figured out. They knew what God did and didn't have to do, what rules God had to live by. But God encountered Job and demolished the formulas. What was Job's reply?

> I know that you are all-powerful: what you conceive, you can perform. I am the man who obscured your designs with my empty-headed words. I have been holding forth on matters I cannot understand, on marvels beyond me and my knowledge. I knew you then only by hearsay; but now, having seen you with my own eyes, I retract all I have said, and in dust and ashes I repent. (Job 42:2-6, JB)

Look what Yahweh said when the Old Testament law became a God-formula.

> What are your endless sacrifices to me? I am sick of the sacrifice of rams and the fat of calves. The blood of bulls and of goats revolts me. When you come to present yourselves before me, who asked you to trample over my courts? Bring me your worthless offerings no more, the smoke of them fills me with disgust. New moons, sabbaths, assemblies—I cannot endure festival and solemnity. Your new moons and your pilgrimages I hate with all my soul. They lay heavy on me. I am tired of bearing them. (Isa. 1:11-14, author's paraphrase)

God's ways of working in history and our lives are odd and surprising. The Lord says, "My thoughts are not your thoughts, neither are my ways your ways . . . As the heavens are higher than the earth, so are my ways higher than your ways and my thoughts than your thoughts" (Isa. 55:8-9, NIV).

God asks Abraham, the father of many nations, to sacrifice his only son; the leper to wash seven times in the Jordan; the army to carry a golden box around Jericho thirteen times and blow on horns; the murderer of believers to become the greatest missionary; the Son of God to die.

Who can pin God down? Abraham thought he knew

God's blueprint—Sarah wouldn't bear a child; Hagar would. The liberated Hebrews had a spiritual plan worked out: if Moses didn't come back soon, they would just make a golden calf to worship instead of God. Moses stuck with the old formula—strike the rock and God will give you water. King Saul thought he understood the program—keep the best of the sheep and cattle to sacrifice to Yahweh. But God was not in any of these things.

Even when God came to earth, people couldn't see it because Jesus didn't fit the formulas. "Can anything good come out of Nazareth?" "Why does he eat with tax collectors and sinners?" "By what authority do you act like this?"

Jesus went out of his way to break the formulas of righteousness. He worked on the Sabbath, touched the unclean, forgave sins, claimed to be God. The religious establishment had God in a box. But Jesus said, "These people honor me with their lips, but their hearts are far from me. The worship they offer me is worthless; the doctrines they teach are only human regulations" (Matt. 15:8-9, author's paraphrase).

Why doesn't God work with formulas? For one thing, God is personal. Formulas work with chemistry and cooking. But they don't work with human beings—not people, not the living God. God is not a life force to be tapped into or a state of being to be attained. God is not even a wise sage dispensing proverbs and prescriptions.

God is relational. God wants encounter. God wants to reveal, to build bonds of love. Relationships with living people are dynamic and alive. Relationship with the living God is even more so.

Another reason God doesn't work with formulas is that God is sovereign, free to do what God pleases. Yahweh is no bellhop who jumps at the snap of our fingers. Yahweh does not perform on demand. We do not conjure up our Savior with magic. No, God is the one who chooses which nations to raise up and when to tear them down. How can you fit this kind of a God into a box?

Perhaps the most important reason God doesn't work with formulas is that we need to walk by faith, not sight (2 Cor. 5:7). Faith and formulas don't mix. If our formulas were 100 percent reliable, we wouldn't need faith; we wouldn't need a living, dynamic relationship with the Lord. Instead of trusting God, we could trust the formulas. But then our belief would become wooden, our growth would come to a halt, and our spirits would turn stale.

God doesn't work with formulas. Neither does life. Life is much too messy and ambiguous to be controlled and understood through formulas.

I've read books that say the answer to every life situation is to praise the Lord. If you break a leg, praise God. If your best friend dies, praise God. If your children are going hungry, praise God. God will reward you and make everything right again.

If only life were that simple. Of course we should often praise God. But other times, we should, like the psalmist, scream at God at the top of our lungs. I think God much prefers that to the silent treatment.

For most of my life, I have told God what I need—with the tacked on phrase "if it be your will." But recently I've entered a phase in which God seems to be saying, "Just shut up. Don't tell me what you need. I will do with your life what I will do. Trust me." Who knows what God will do? And who knows how long it will be before it's time again to ask for things myself?

Life is a journey, not a designed system. Walking with God is an adventure, not a program. There are no hard and fast blueprints. No procedures to guarantee success. There is only the wisdom of experience, the hope of faith, and the risk of relationship.

In C. S. Lewis' children's story *The Silver Chair*, Jill, a little girl from our world, accidentally stumbles into the world of Narnia. She is extremely thirsty and comes on a stream. But a Lion, Aslan, is sitting by the stream. She is terrified. Aslan says to her, "If you are thirsty, you may drink." She doesn't move.

"Are you not thirsty?" said the Lion.

"I'm dying of thirst," said Jill.

"Then drink," said the Lion.

"May I—could I—would you mind going away while I do?" said Jill.

The Lion answered this only by a look and a very low growl. And, as Jill gazed at its motionless bulk, she realized that she might as well have asked a whole mountain to move aside for her convenience.

The delicious rippling noise of the stream was driving her nearly frantic.

"Will you promise not to—do anything to me, if I do come?" said Jill.

"I make no promise," said the Lion.

Jill was so thirsty now that, without noticing it, she had come a step nearer.

"Do you eat girls?" she asked.

"I have swallowed up girls and boys, women and men, kings and emperors, cities and realms," said the Lion. It didn't say this as if it were boasting, nor as if it were sorry, nor as if it were angry. It just said it.

"I daren't come and drink," said Jill.

"Then you will die of thirst," said the Lion.

"Oh dear!" said Jill, coming another step nearer. "I suppose I must go and look for another stream then."

"There is no other stream," said the Lion.

It never occurred to Jill to disbelieve the Lion—no one who had seen his stern face could do that—and her mind suddenly made itself up. It was the worst thing she had ever had to do, but she went forward to the stream, knelt down, and began scooping water in her hand. It was the coldest, most refreshing water she had ever tasted. You didn't need to drink much of it, for it quenched your thirst at once. Before she tasted it she had been intending to make a dash away from the Lion the moment she finished. Now she realized that this would be, on the whole, the most dangerous thing of all. She got up and stood there with her lips still wet from drinking.

What a picture of the Christ we serve: a dangerous, uncaged lion! We don't bargain or negotiate with God. We surrender our lives. We don't exercise tidy God-formulas. We encounter a living relationship.

The heavenly, benevolent grandparent who doles out candy at our request is a figment of our imagination. The Living One laughs and shakes the foundation of our lives to wake us from dreaming. To our God-in-a-box theologies, God says, "Don't play games with me." To our trustworthy formulas, "Forget them and walk with me." And to our recipes for spiritual success, "Just give me your lives."

God is elusive—too slippery to be pinned down or forced into a mold. You expect to find God in a mighty wind, an earthquake, a fire. Instead God comes in the gentle whisper (1 Kings 19:9-14). You expect God in the holy temple or the courts of the mighty. But more likely God is at a party with sinners or in a burning bush or walking next to you to Emmaus. Yet you might not know it, and you certainly can't count on it. Wrap your fingers around God and you'll have nothing.

Like Jill, we want assurance. We want security. We want our life with Christ to be safe and predictable. But if we really want to know God and want to grow, we must let go of our formulas and step out in the risk of faith. Yes, the lion is scary, but the other option is to die of thirst.

An Alternative for Transcendence Junkies

The next thing we need to consider, as we rethink spirituality, is that ordinary, everyday life is itself very spiritual.

The people in my community like to eat together. Not too long ago we had a potluck breakfast before worship. Somebody made pancakes and brought along with them some authentic, 100 percent Vermont maple syrup—that rare, real stuff that comes from maple trees. I sat down with a steaming stack covered in melted butter and plenty of Vermont's finest, ready for an authentic, exciting taste.

I didn't like it. It didn't taste right. While scanning the food table to see if anyone had brought the grocery-store-version syrup, I realized how ridiculous I was being. All my life I had poured maple-flavored corn syrup on pancakes. Now I had the real thing—and didn't want it. I had grown so fond of the imitation that I didn't enjoy the reality.

This happens with Christians. We develop expectations about what God should be like, what church should be like, what the Christian life should be like. These expectations often aren't true to reality. Then when we meet the reality, we don't recognize or appreciate it.

Take the everyday, routine, ordinary, secular part of our lives, for example. Here is an aspect of life very important in God's economy of creation and salvation. Yet many Christians think, feel, and act as if the everyday part of life is somehow disconnected from the spiritual part.

One typical consequence of this mistaken splitting of the sacred and the secular is the compartmentalization of spiritual life. We come to recognize God's work in our lives only when we experience (for lack of a better phrase) powerful spiritual feelings.

Rather than comprehending and appreciating the Spirit of God in our *everyday* lives, we cast about to find God in spiritual highs. We become transcendence junkies. We go to the church with the dynamic preacher who can "touch our hearts" week in and week out. We consume Christian best-sellers, hoping one will move us. We frequent Christian retreats, seminars, and conferences to keep our spiritual engines hot. Some Christians even become disciples of flashy television preachers who promise all manner of healing, power, miracles, and spiritual experiences (as long as the lucre keeps flowing in).

Not all these things are bad. Neither is chocolate fudge. But we wouldn't be healthy if we ate chocolate fudge three meals a day, every day. And we certainly won't be healthy if we ask "profound spiritual feelings" to satisfy our desire to know and experience God in our lives. Spiritual highs should be the dessert, not the main course, of discipleship.

Unlike fudge, powerful spiritual experiences and feelings cannot be bought at a candy store and consumed in a few minutes. They take time and energy. In the meantime there are groceries to be bought, cars to be fixed, children to be attended to, incomes to be earned.

We would do well to stop chasing spiritual highs and begin developing the eyes to see and the heart to appreciate God in the everyday. Our routine, normal lives must be relevant to God's work, connected to knowledge of our Creator, significant to the in-breaking of the kingdom. These connections only are woven as we develop and internalize a spirituality of everyday life.

The point is not to be satisfied with mundane life drained of spiritual meaning. The point is to learn to recognize the spiritual significance of everyday existence.

Everyday Life Spirituality

A spirituality of everyday life is gradually gaining more attention today but is still underdeveloped in Christian theology. There are many more problems and questions than solutions and answers. Still, such a spirituality begs to be brought to maturity. To this end, it may be worth reflecting on two basic questions. One focuses on God's creation, the other on God's redemption. First, what gives glory to God? Second, how does God sanctify us?

What gives glory to God? The chief purpose of our existence is to glorify God. For that end we were created and are being redeemed. Then how do we give glory to God? Spread the gospel? Sing songs of worship? Minister to the needy? Yes—but there are also other ways.

The story of creation helps us see what humans can do for God's glory. God placed humans in a garden to cultivate and keep it (Gen. 2:15). God said, "Flourish and multiply, fill the earth and cultivate it; take care of the fish of the sea and the birds of the sky, and over every thing that is alive. Look, I have given you every plant and tree that is on the earth to be food for you" (Gen. 1:28-29, author's paraphrase). God saw that what had been made was very good. Creation glorified the creator.

What was the God-glorifying task given to humans? To escape the world through spiritual contemplation? To transcend the ordinary with spiritual highs? No. Our job on this earth, the thing that best glorifies our Creator, is "worldly," material, fleshy. We are to watch over the garden—our natural and social environment. We are to care for and nurture it. We are to reproduce, have children, make families. What best glorifies the Creator is this: the living of ordinary life (including family life, agriculture, conservation, economic and commercial endeavors) by people in right relationship with God.

Notice how God instructed the people to live, even as God's discipline sent them into exile in Babylon.

> Build houses and settle down; plant gardens and eat what they produce. Marry and have sons and daughters; find

> wives for your sons and give your daughters in marriage, so that they too may have sons and daughters. Increase in number there; do not decrease. Also, seek the peace and prosperity of the city to which I have carried you into exile. Pray to the Lord for it, because if it prospers, you too will prosper. (Jer. 29:5-7, NIV)

Most of our lives are filled with the tasks of producing and reproducing—working, eating, sleeping, raising families, and so on. These are not simply routine necessities that are ultimately secular and devoid of spiritual value. They are the core of the divine mandate God has given us. They represent the very thing that God charged humans to accomplish for God's glory.

This is why Paul exhorts believers, "Whether you eat or drink or whatever you do, do all to the glory of God" (1 Cor. 10:31, RSV). Notice Paul didn't say, "Do those thing which glorify God." No, Paul said, "In all things glorify God."

Paul clearly didn't view life as having two parts, the sacred and the secular (with the secular being somehow less important or glorifying to God). Rather, Paul knew that every human activity, including *everyday* activities—perhaps *especially* everyday activities like eating and drinking—can and should glorify God.

We turn now to the second question. How does God sanctify us? At the heart of the Christian story is the knowledge that we, our relationships, and the world are not okay (transactional analysis notwithstanding). Something is profoundly wrong with the way things are.

The good news, however, is that God is making things right. God is renewing the heavens and the earth. And God is working in us and our relationships to heal our brokenness, to rehumanize us, to roll back the power of sin in our lives. In traditional theological language, God is sanctifying us.

But how does this happen? How does God accomplish this great redemptive work of making us the people God wants us to be? Through swift, radical character-transformation? By spectacular miracles? With bolts of lightning and pillars of fire? Perhaps sometimes, but generally not. For the most part, our sanctification happens in and through the workings of our everyday lives, gradually, over time.

Sanctification is not something we achieve by escaping our ordinary lives. Quite the contrary, God is weaving together the decisions, events, pressures, routines, crises, and responsibilities of our ordinary, everyday lives to help us change and grow. Everyday life is not a *hindrance* to God's work in our lives. It is the *primary* way God works in our lives.

But if this is so, why don't we more clearly see God working in the everyday? Why does it *feel* so unspiritual, so ordinary? Perhaps because it seems God does not often work in the open. For some reason, God prefers to keep hidden, behind the bushes, as it were. With a few exceptions, Jesus' habit of declining fame and attention (Mark 1:43-44; 7:36; 9:30) seems to represent God's typical style of working to redeem the world.

Consequently, it often takes the distance of years to understand God's work in our lives. We can often see how God worked to heal and grow us the past. But who knows exactly what God is doing with us today? This can be difficult. When we want to know God's will, God is often silent. When we demand to understand the meaning of life's hard times, God often does not answer. Yet God is there, working to heal us.

Think of Joseph. Betrayed and enslaved by his brothers. Unjustly imprisoned by his employer. Forgotten by the fellow inmates he helped. Yet as Joseph only later realized, God was busy the whole time (Gen. 45:5-8).

But did Joseph understand the purpose of God while he was marching off as a slave, or falsely accused of rape, or sitting in a cold jail? To him, I'm sure, his troubles felt anything but spiritual, anything but the place God was at work.

Sometimes unexpectedly we do catch a fleeting glimpse, a hint of God's hand. But the glimpse soon passes, the hint slips away. Life again becomes normal. We are wise simply to smile at God's craftiness, believe God is with us, and embrace the everyday in all its spirituality.

We can glorify God through everyday tasks. And we participate in God's healing sanctification through everyday circumstances and events. We can either see God in the everyday or focus only on the spiritually spectacular. We can learn to recognize and appreciate reality or we can allow our distorted expectations to drive us toward something else.

It may not be worth it for me to cultivate a taste for authentic, Vermont maple syrup; the grocery store version is more available and less costly. Everyday life, however, is very available. And since everyday life is such an important arena for God's work of redemption, it is costly *not* to cultivate and live out a spirituality of everyday life.

The Eternal Significance of the Little and Ordinary

Transcendence junkies are incessantly chasing after the spiritually big and spectacular. But in God's upside-down kingdom, often big is really not big—but little. And little is big. In God's foolish wisdom, apparently insignificant deeds are actually eternally significant. Small matters are actually pregnant with ultimate importance.

The Gospel of Matthew portrays this paradoxical truth clearly. To call someone a fool is to invite hellfire (Matt 5:21-22). But simply to give a cup of cold water to a child brings eternal reward (Matt 10:42). The little throwaway words we speak will vindicate or condemn us on the day of judgment (Matt 12:36-37). And what we decide here on earth will be decided in heaven (Matt 16:19, 18:18).

Simply to welcome a child is, in fact, to welcome Christ himself (Matt 18:5), just as care for a person who is hungry, thirsty, outcast, naked, sick, or in prison is to do the same for the eternal King of glory (Matt 25:31-46). Faithfulness in the little things of our everyday lives determines how worthy we are for heavenly responsibilities (Matt. 24:45-47, 25:14-23).

God seems to enjoy hiding the eternally profound in the tiny. Indeed, our redemption through the cross—an ignominious death in an unimportant corner of the world—is foolish and weak in the world's eyes. But it is the power of cosmic salvation in God's plan (1 Cor. 1:18-25). Similarly the kingdom of God is, at first, like the tiny mustard seed. But eventually it grows into an enormous, life-giving tree (Matt. 13:31-32).

The point is not to become introspectively uptight about every detail of our lives. Quite the opposite. We can live in freedom and joy, for God our loving parent is glad to give us the kingdom (Luke 12:32). The point here is to recognize and take courage in this promise: the simplest acts of love, the smallest words of kindness, the most ordinary deeds of faithfulness are the things out of which eternity is built. It is ordinary, everyday life more than the spiritually dramatic that opens doors to God's reign. That is a truth that ought to form our spirituality.

It's Good to Be Human

Another part of a spirituality of everyday life involves embracing our humanness. By the sound of some popular spiritualities, you would think God wants to turn us into bored spirits. We know God wants us to become holy. But in many spiritualities that seems to mean we become unearthly, pious divinities. We know God wants to sanctify us. But sometimes that sounds like we'll end up bland, semi-dazed milk-toasts. Can't you just see it—glowing faces, perpetual smiles, weak handshakes, and halos?

The problem is most of us don't want to become any of these things. We don't want to become otherworldly monks or oh-so-pious saints. We want to dig into life, to involve ourselves in the world. We want to get our feet dirty. I myself feel much more comfortable with concrete and ice cream and flesh and soil. Who wants to be a robed spirit, even if you do shine and sing great hymns?

In fact, such spiritualities are misinformed. Their images of holiness, sanctification, and perfection are misguided. God doesn't want to turn us into bored, pious divinities. God wants to change us back into what God meant us to be, which is whole, healthy human beings.

God liked the world God created. And the part God liked best were the humans. Adam and Eve were perfect—whole, healthy, and happy. They laughed, ate, and got dirt under their toenails.

Yet how many times have you heard the expression "I'm sorry, but I'm only human" (which really translates, "Don't expect too much out of me because I'm a real mess")? Being human doesn't mean being a mess. To be human is good.

Right now, however, we're not truly human—we're distortions of what is really human. We're twisted versions of what God created us to be, not the real thing. If we were truly human, we wouldn't use our humanness as an excuse for our failures.

Being human is good. But because we so often associate it with our present twisted state, we end up thinking this fleshly, earthy, human existence is itself bad. So naturally we picture holiness as somehow escaping our humanity. But we're wrong.

If we want to know what God wants us to be, what our ideal state looks like, we have an example—Jesus of Nazareth. Jesus is the one example in history of a real human being. He was like the humans God created in the garden, without sin, undistorted by its power.

What was Jesus like? One thing is sure. He was no unearthly, pious apparition. He was as human as you get. He ate fish, drank wine, laughed. He slept, felt emotions, became tired, got sweaty. He was male, a sexual being. Being human was not a problem for Jesus. It was not something he tried to escape.

Nor did Jesus try to escape the world. He did not separate himself from certain people or places. He felt comfortable at a wedding party and in the temple. He spoke with authorities and peasants, priests and riffraff, rich and poor, in markets, fields, boats, streets, living rooms, and deserts. Jesus was at home in the physical world.

God made us human because God wanted to. Our sin has not changed that. God still wants us to be human. The gospel does not save us *from* humanness but into *fuller* humanness. Becoming righteous does not mean escaping but restoring our human existence. Sin dehumanizes us; the gospel rehumanizes us. To become holy is to become truly human.

What exactly does a truly healthy, authentic human look like? Two passages in Scripture help us. First, in Matthew 22:34-40 Jesus commanded two things: to love God and to love others as ourselves. That's it. No list of do's and don'ts. No system of legal regulations or programs to follow. Simply love God and other people.

Second, in Galatians 5:22 Paul describes what righteous people look like. They are characterized by love, joy, peace, patience, kindness, goodness, gentleness, trustfulness, and self-control.

These are the marks of a whole, healthy human being. They describe what Jesus was like. They tell us what we are to become.

By Grace Alone

The heart and foundation of this spirituality of everyday life is the recognition that God has fully and eternally justified us by grace alone, through faith. Thus whatever form and texture this spirituality takes, it has nothing to do with the question of our justification and adoption into the family of God.

Many legalistic spiritualities today act as if we determine how God feels about us by how we act. But we do not turn God's love for us on and off like a light bulb, depending on how "good" we are. Hence we waste time if we continually, introspectively take our spiritual temperature.

The issues of sin and guilt were resolved on the cross. Our salvation is a matter of God purposefully taking hold of our lives, not of our fearfully grasping for or earning God's acceptance. We *are* accepted *and* justified. We should move on into life with that confidence.

True spirituality, then, does not mean keeping God on our good side. It means growing in love, wisdom, maturity, commitment, and childlikeness in our everyday lives. It means becoming sensitized to the things in life that make God laugh and weep, then laughing and weeping with God. True spirituality means having the values and goals of the kingdom of God so saturate our beings that our own everyday thoughts and feelings, attitudes and desires, express God's in-breaking reign.

Another word of caution: a spirituality of everyday life should not be used as a rationalization for avoiding the traditional spiritual disciplines of prayer, Scripture reading, meditation, and so on. For these disciplines are the rich soil out of which true everyday-life spirituality grows. Only by opening ourselves to God's Word and Spirit do we come to see God working on the everyday.

A grace-ful spirituality of everyday life is not the dominant spirituality in Christian circles today. Neither is it well developed. There are many questions and issues to be worked out in theory and practice. The ideas of this chapter are only preliminary steps. Nevertheless, such a spirituality of everyday life begs to be cultivated and brought to maturity as we seek to go to the root and find renewal.

7

Practice Lifestyle Evangelism

WHEN I WAS a teenager, I belonged to a vibrant church that was big on evangelism. Even at that age, I would go with a team into downtown Philadelphia, stand on the granite subway stations, and preach the gospel. Some people stopped briefly, gave us blank stares, and moved on. A few tried to shout us down or argued with us. I thought what I was doing was good, and maybe it was.

But even then I had nagging doubts and questions. Were we making any connection with these pedestrians? Was what we were saying at all meaningful to them? Was it right to come in from the outside and intrude into their lives in that way? Was this the best way to communicate the gospel?

Radical church renewal challenges the church to spread the good news of God's reign. But evangelism these days is tough. People just don't seem to want to hear the gospel. They throw our tracts on the sidewalk, slam doors in our faces, maybe even jeer at us as we share our good news.

People ignore our evangelistic efforts. They just sit in front of the television (cheese-doodles in hand), go to the shopping mall (credit card in hand), and go out to parties (vodka in hand). Such a culture needs the gospel. So why don't people listen?

Techniques That Trivialize

The problem is not that many Christians don't evangelize. A glance through popular Christian magazines reveals all kinds of available, neat evangelistic techniques.

For some people, wearing Christian jewelry is popular (in gold or silver—a subtle way to put your money where your mouth is). Christian clothes are popular too. There's nothing like wearing a Jesus Battalion or Christian Commando T-shirt to let them know for whom you're fighting. Or how about Christian bank checks? Share the Word with sixteen people every time you spend money!

Bumper stickers are popular too. I've seen everything from the enigmatic Wise Men Still Seek Him to the daring Commit a Death Defying Act: Accept Christ. Some churches use direct-mail campaigns—just like Madison Avenue. Another creative "tract" is the Born Again Birth Certificate (which doubles as a fund raiser).

Church-based evangelism is popular too. According to magazine ads, you can entice nonbelievers into church buildings by replacing the old hard pews with padded ones (you've got to be comfortable to believe the gospel, right?). Then you can show a Bible story film or two. In fact, you can show the whole Bible if you want to (fifteen films, twenty minutes each). Of course, television evangelism is the ultimate—reach millions with the gospel, and for a fraction of the cost per contact.

Yet with all these innovative evangelism techniques, people still don't seem to be listening when we preach the gospel. Not even with our best T-shirts and television shows. Slick techniques, it seems, are not the answer.

I suspect slick techniques are not only not the answer—they are part of the problem. For a long time I wondered why people don't listen when Christians evangelize. Then I had a discomforting thought. Maybe they *are* listening, all too well. Maybe they are hearing exactly what we are saying and finding nothing of value in it. Not because the gospel has nothing of value, but because they can't hear the real gospel above the noise of our message.

Our slick techniques don't communicate the gospel but a trivialized caricature. What we display on our bumper stickers and belt buckles and bank checks and buttons is not the real gospel. It is a weak and silly rendition of the gospel. So it may be pointless to ask why people don't accept the gospel—they never really hear it in the first place.

The gospel of God's kingdom is indeed simple. But it is not just simple. It is also very deep. Notice that Jesus did not have a tidy message. It took three years and a lot of parables and stories to paint a picture of the kingdom of God. Can we communicate this richness with a T-shirt logo or a one-minute run through a tract?

Further, it's not just a matter of somehow squeezing the "complete" gospel onto a bumper sticker. Even if we could do that through some wonder of miniaturization, the gospel would still be trivialized. The reason is that the essence of *what* is communicated is radically affected by *how* it is communicated. Thus the gospel on television communicates differently than through a book. And differently again through a song. Communication media—whether smoke signals or MTV or Morse code—have an impact on the message.

What happens to the gospel when we stick it on a chrome bumper or give it away on a tacky Born Again Birth Certificate? What happens when we try to encapsulate it in a God-has-a-perfect-plan-for-your-life pitch to a pedestrian? It becomes, despite all good intentions, trivialized, banal, petty. What is communicated is unavoidably a misrepresentation of the real thing. It's no wonder people don't want any part of it.

Another problem is that we stole our evangelistic techniques from people who market laundry detergents and automobiles. The techniques themselves make the gospel seem as worldly as anything it is supposed to save people from. The good news becomes another product among far too many other products. People assume we are offering only more of what they already have

Think for a moment about what we do. We say our world is lost and needs salvation. Then we go out of our way to dress the good news in the same clothes as Wisk and Charmin. We make it appear that Christianity is just another of the long line of products offering whiter whites, sex appeal, and oh-what-a-feeling.

Who are we kidding? Ours is a hollow and wearisome society, a culture of canned laughter and passing pop stars. So why are we so eager to emulate it? Why are we intent on commercializing ourselves with Good News Videos, Crystal Cathedrals, Heritage USAs, Direct Mail Outreach, 700 Clubs, and the rest? Do we think imitating the problem will solve it?

When we take our cues from Hollywood and Madison Avenue, we shouldn't be surprised if people respond to our snazzy evangelism methods with a yawn. Can "ClergyCard" take on MasterCard and win? Can Heritage USA take on Disney World and win? Through our direct-mail evangelism we jump into a sea of direct-mail trash, where we are drowned by Publisher's Clearinghouse and the rest. Our methods match the world's in worldliness and banality—and we wonder why the power of the gospel gets lost.

What are we after in our evangelism anyway? A raised hand during altar-calls? A walk down the aisle? A repeat-after-me prayer? What relation do these things have to true conversion, a new way of living, Christian discipleship?

The good news is also difficult news. It calls us to become slaves to righteousness and justice, to lay down our lives, to take up our crosses, to put to death our old nature. But our Madison Avenue techniques allure people into the church with promises of fulfillment and pleasure. Then we are puzzled when, ten years later, they are still spiritual babies. Could it be that the fruit of our mod evangelism is as meaningful as the new lemon-fresh scent in our dish detergent?

If we were honest, we would see that much of our evangelism is dishonest. We tell people becoming Christian will make them happy. God has wonderful plans for their lives. Things will get better if they only accept Jesus into their hearts. All true, in a way. But it also makes the gospel sound like just another competing commodity. If the good news is different than Kitchen Magician, maybe we ought to speak of it in a different way.

The world has plenty of itself, actually. It does not need us to join the ranks of Cap'n Crunch and Mr. Clean. It needs something different. It needs and longs for something challenging, something deeply satisfying, something that cuts through the glitter of Hollywood and Madison Avenue. Underneath the glitter, many people yearn, not for what is cheap and easy, but for what is meaningful—even if challenging and difficult. To win the world by aping the world is self-defeating.

Don't Tell Me, Show Me

The Bible helps us see where we went wrong. For the Bible makes it clear that the central and irreplaceable medium for communicating the gospel is the quality of believers' lives together.

Jesus' last message to his followers was: "Love one another; just as I have loved you, you also must love one another. Everyone will know that you are my disciples if you love one another" (John 13:34-35, author's paraphrase). Actions, apparently, speak louder than words. The lives of people who genuinely love each other, for all their warts and false starts, will be a truer explanation of the good news than the most precisely pitched evangelistic message.

Peter urges Christians to, "as aliens and strangers in the world, abstain from sinful desires. . . . Live such good lives among the pagans that, though they accuse you of doing wrong, they may see your good deeds and glorify God" (1 Pet. 2:11-12, author's paraphrase). Likewise, Paul urges the Corinthians to conduct themselves so that when an unbeliever sees them, "he will fall down and worship God, exclaiming, 'God is really among you!' " (1 Cor. 14:25, NIV).

I recently heard of a Christian smoker who tried hard to keep his smoking hidden so that it wouldn't "ruin his testimony." Not only does this kind of attitude lose sight of priorities (smoking is ruining his lungs more than his testimony), it presumes nonbelievers can be tricked into the kingdom by lives without substance. In fact, the world is not fooled or impressed by facades of righteousness.

Would we, in our evangelistic programs, like to see new believers every day? Let's look at how it happened in the early church.

> These remained faithful to the teaching of the apostles, to the brotherhood, to the breaking of the bread and to prayers. The many miracles and signs worked through the

apostles made a deep impression on everyone. The faithful all lived together and owned everything in common; they sold their goods and possessions and shared out the proceeds among themselves according to what each one needed. They went as a body to the Temple every day but met in their houses for the breaking of bread; they shared their food gladly and generously; they praised God and were looked up to by everyone. Day by day the Lord added to their community those destined to be saved. (Acts 2:42-47, JB; also see 4:32-35)

No Christian bumper stickers here. They simply lived authentically redeemed lives in community. The depth of that life did its own communicating.

Luke goes to great lengths to tell how Peter and John got to preach to the people at the temple and to the Sanhedrin (Acts 3:1—4:31). They didn't entice the people into their church buildings with comfortable pews and films. They didn't even intend to preach at all, but simply to pray.

However, "it happened that . . ." (3:2, JB). Peter and John were simply living as channels of God's healing love. It was only *after* this act of healing and love that they preached—as an *explanation* of what had happened. Evangelism flowed naturally from living out the transforming power of the kingdom of God. No slick techniques were necessary.

Biblical evangelism, then, is not cornering people and confronting them with the gospel. Nor is it charming people with a sweet, easy pseudo-gospel. Biblical evangelism is first incarnating the reign of God in community, then answering the inevitable questions: "Why do you live the way you do? What motivates you to live so differently?"

Peter wrote, "In your hearts set apart Christ as Lord, and always be prepared to give an answer to everyone who asks you to give a reason for the hope that you have" (1 Pet. 3:15, author's paraphrase).

When I first worked on developing my writing skills, a composition teacher offered me a simple maxim: "Don't tell me, show me." That maxim is also the best advice for churches interested in responsible and effective evangelism. The world is sick and tired of being told about Jesus. The world needs to be *shown* Jesus.

As Christ was God incarnate, God in flesh and blood living in obedience to his parent, so we the church are to be Christ incarnate. We are to be Christ's body, living out in flesh and blood the reign of God. This is a difficult project for marketing agents, but it's the basic calling of God's people.

Sometimes our kingdom lifestyles can bear witness without our intending it. For the past eight years, my wife and I have lived in cooperatively owned, multifamily houses with others in our community. A few years ago we and another family wanted to move together to a new neighborhood.

Our realtor was amazed. "I have never seen cooperative housing last for more than one house!" she exclaimed. "What's your secret?"

Right then, in a way that would have never happened had I simply handed her an evangelistic tract, I had the opportunity to explain something about the kingdom. "The reason why we live this way is because. . . ."

It is time to abandon our high-tech evangelistic outreaches, pull the plugs on the television programs, and peel off our Christian bumper stickers. Having fired our Madison Avenue consultants and dumped our direct-mail schemes, we can get back to basics. We can communicate the gospel by the witness of our lives. That means focusing our energies on becoming more fully the people of God. It means living lives which are so obviously influenced by an encounter with God that no one can find another reasonable explanation for us.

Danger: Works-Righteousness

A brief word of warning is needed, however, to avoid deadly self-righteousness. The day people start asking us "Why do you live so differently?" is the day we have the right to tell the good news. But it would be a fatal mistake to then focus on our "good works." Jesus said,

> You are the light of the world. A city on a hill cannot be hidden. Neither do people light a lamp and put it under a bowl. Instead they put it on a stand, and it gives light to everyone in the house. In the same way, let your light shine before others, that they may see your good deeds and praise your Father in heaven. (Matt. 5:14-16, author's paraphrase)

Lifestyle evangelism must shine the spotlight on God, not us. It must result in God's praise, not ours. If our lives have been transformed at all, it is because of God's grace and God's grace alone. Indeed, the good news itself is that only God's grace frees us to live a new life of faith and discipleship. While what we have to *show* is what God has done in our lives, what we have to *tell* is that only God can do it.

Living a Contrast Culture

Evangelism is explaining to the world why we Christians live differently. But few people today are asking the church, "Why do you live so differently?" They have no reason to ask. For the lifestyles of the majority of churchgoers in this country are often almost identical to the lifestyles of those who have nothing to do with church. The only difference, usually, is a thin spiritual veneer brushed on the surface, a religious frosting on a worldly cake.

Many Christians place great legalistic, spiritual importance on abstinence from relatively *trivial* things (from dancing to movies to swearing to card playing to mowing the lawn on Sundays). This is because Christians aren't much different than others in relation to *important* things (basic values and behavior concerning wealth, power, prestige, justice, security, peace, work, time).

Christians know they should be different from the world *in some way*—otherwise, what would Christianity mean? So, in an effort to establish some kind of Christian distinctiveness, they focus on the trivial. And the trivial is that which does not require us to make difficult changes in our lives.

In the end, it is okay to be entirely captive to the idols of mass-consumerism as long as we don't watch R-rated movies. It is acceptable to spend our entire lives pursuing a cozy, suburban affluence as long as we don't mow the lawn on Sunday. It is just fine to live a life completely indifferent to world poverty and hunger as long as we don't drink liquor. Like the Pharisees, we "strain out the gnat and swallow the camel" (Matt. 23:24, author's paraphrase).

Sure the world sees that church people are nice. But does it see deeply committed, sacrificial love in Christian community? It may be evident that most Christians don't swear. But is it clear that the people of God are more dedicated to justice for the poor than to accumulating ever greater amounts of power and prestige?

Christians are fond of saying this world needs Jesus. But if Jesus doesn't really change us, what is it the world needs? What fundamental changes should anyone expect Jesus will make in the world when Jesus appears not to have made fundamental changes in the corporate lives of believers?

Is it any wonder our evangelism becomes more banal every year? The church does not concretely demonstrate the meaning of the gospel in an alternative way of life— one that incarnates the values and commitments of the kingdom of God. Thus it is forced to sell the gospel (or whatever is left of it) to the world with trite slogans, hackneyed tracts, and nauseating television shows.

The point is not that the church should be a counter-culture, because we're not *against* the world. We're very much for the world. We should be a *contrast* culture, one that concretely and visibly highlights the differences between life according to the kingdom of God and life according to the kingdom of the world. People should be able to look at the church and say, "Oh, so *that's* the difference Jesus makes in human life!"

But instead of living a contrast culture, church goers often work hard to justify their willingness to absorb the very assumptions, values, and lifestyles the gospel is supposed to confront, redeem, and transform.

For Example

Let's shift gears now and explore, for example, mass-consumer materialism. Our socioeconomic system is designed to produce and consume enormous amounts of stuff. It is common in our society for people to singlemindedly dream, live, learn, and work for endless hours simply to accumulate more and more wealth and possessions. As billionaire John D. Rockefeller quipped, "How much money is enough? Just a little bit more."

But the Bible says that material wealth and the pursuit of it has the almost irresistible tendency to become an idol for individuals and nations. It deceptively displaces God as God, ruins spiritual lives, and violates the cause of justice.

According to the Bible, material prosperity has the tendency to make us forget about God (Deut. 8:11-14, 17-18). It is extremely difficult for a rich person to be a Christian at all (Luke 18:24-25; Matt. 19:23-24; Mark 10:23). The desire for money leads people to ruin and destroys their faith (1 Tim. 6:9-10). The hunger for material things is a major cause of fighting and wars (James 4:1-2). Material abundance blinds people to the needy people around them and leads them to damnation (Luke 16:19-31). Possessions become the objects of our trust and affection, destroying our trust in and love for God (Luke 12:16-21). Greedy people will not be part of God's coming kingdom (Eph. 5:5; 1 Cor. 6:9-10).

The litany continues. Possessions are the prime candidate for displacing God in our lives (Matt. 6:24). We should be fundamentally unconcerned about our material needs, money, and possessions (Matt. 6:25-34; Luke 12:22-31, 33-34, Heb. 13:5) Joining God's kingdom entails, for some if not for all, selling some or all of one's possessions and giving to the poor (Luke 12:33-34; Luke 19:8-9; Matt. 19:16-22). Love of money makes one inclined not to take Jesus seriously (Luke 16:14). Riches deceive us, choking the Word of God from our lives (Matt. 13:22).

Clearly wealth is a great, if not *the* greatest, threat to human spiritual well-being—even salvation. Yet Christians justify their conformity to the cultural pursuit of wealth with tired, old rationalizations: "It's okay to own all this as long as, in my heart, I would be willing to part with it if I had to." "But someone has to be rich to evangelize the rich." "Even the Bible says, 'The poor you will always have with you,' so why be concerned with poverty?" "But I tithe 10 percent (so the rest is mine)." "Prosperity is God's blessing for me to enjoy."

In the end, in the spiritually profound area of wealth and possessions, Christians look no different than other idolatrous, materialistic American-dream-seekers. The alternative values of the kingdom are rationalized away. God's people conform to the ways of the world. And the power of the church's evangelism evaporates.

The church *could* act differently. Christians could stop behaving like alcoholics in denial. They could cease overestimating their own ability to resist and control wealth's seductive power. Christians could stop conforming to the pattern of the world and be transformed to demonstrate God's will (Rom. 12:2). Christians could take the Bible seriously and begin to shape a community way of life according to the values of the kingdom.

Believers in Christian community could step off the accumulation conveyor belt. They could choose a modest standard of living, giving away their surplus to those in need. Believers could live according to the principle of sufficiency, avoiding poverty and luxury (1 Tim. 6:8-10; Prov. 30:8-9). God's people in community could generously share their wealth with one another, as they are able, when any needs arise (see Acts 2:43-47; 4:32-37; 5:1-11; 6:1-7).

In these ways, Christians could work toward relative equality among the people of God, just as Paul taught (2 Cor. 8:13-15). Christians could cultivate in their communities genuinely carefree, joyful, contented dealings with money (Matt. 6:25-33). Instead of practicing conspicuous consumption, believers in community could practice conspicuous contentment—and even some healthy, voluntary downward mobility.

The community of believers at Reba Place Fellowship in Evanston, Illinois, has chosen to do exactly this. Members of Reba Place share their money in a common purse. They pool paychecks, own houses and cars in common, and live in extended family-like households. To live simply and in solidarity with the poor, they have voluntarily chosen to consume at a Chicago poverty-line standard. The rest of their money they spend on service and ministry.

Half of the community members work in the paid labor force to support the community. Many are in teaching, nursing, social work, and other human service fields. The other half work at homemaking or in community-sponsored ministries, such as a neighborhood nursery school, a halfway-house for the mentally ill, a prison, and a refugee ministry.

No one lives in luxury, no one lives in poverty, everyone takes care of everyone. Everyone works to serve God and not mammon in their hearts. This is how the believers at Reba Place Fellowship show with their lives the joyful renunciation of the mass-consumer materialism idol.

Living a contrast culture with money doesn't necessarily require being this radical, however. Many Christian communities don't actually pool paychecks. But they do follow other alternative economic practices. These might include progressive tithing, no-interest housing loans, cooperative ownership of consumer durables, and lifestyle-accountability discussion groups.

The issue of mass-consumer materialism is only one example of how the church should live a contrast culture and how the church can practice lifestyle evangelism. There are many other possibilities. By living a contrast culture in these and other ways, the church can concretely and visibly declare to the world the gospel of the kingdom of God.

People will ask, "Why do you live that way?" We can answer, "Because the reign of God has broken into our lives and has freed us from the ways of the world!" Then we can invite those people to let the reign of God break into and change *their* lives. *That* is lifestyle evangelism at work.

Suppose we disciples of Jesus were to devote ourselves, by God's grace, truly to becoming the family of God. Suppose we did so with anything like the intensity and extensiveness of the early church. Then the problem might not be figuring out how to entice reluctant people into our churches. It might be figuring out what to do with all the people who sincerely want to live a new way of life in Christ. Wouldn't that be a nice problem to have?

8

Work for Social Justice

RADICAL CHURCH RENEWAL seeks to change not only our attitudes, church structures, and spiritualities. It also seeks to transform the way we engage ourselves as churches with the fallen social order. Radical church renewal calls us to work for social justice.

Social Justice Is Christian Business

As children of God, one way we know how we ought to think and live is by learning the character and concerns of God and making them ours. As God our heavenly parent loves, so should we love. As God forgives, so should we forgive. As God is righteous, so should we be.

One characteristic of God that Christians often neglect however, is that God loves and demands justice in human society. God calls God's people to struggle for social justice. This can be seen throughout the Bible.

God loves justice. God has a passion for and delights in justice. "The Lord is righteous, he loves justice" (Ps. 11:7, NIV). "The Lord loves righteousness and justice" (Ps.

33:5, NIV). "The Lord loves justice" (Ps. 37:28, author's paraphrase) "The King is mighty, he loves justice; he has established equity and has done what is just" (Ps. 99:4, author's paraphrase). "The Lord is a God of justice" (Isa. 30:18, NIV). "I, the Lord, loves justice" (Isa. 61:8, NIV). "Let him who boasts boast about this: that he understands and knows me, that I am the Lord who exercises kindness, justice and righteousness on earth, for in these I delight" (Jer. 9:24, NIV).

Not only does God love and delight in justice. God works in history to establish justice. "God executes justice for the fatherless and widow, and loves foreigners, giving them food and clothing" (Deut. 10:18-19, author's paraphrase). "God rises up to establish justice for all the oppressed of the earth" (Ps. 76:9, author's paraphrase). "The Lord works vindication and justice for all who are oppressed" (Ps. 103:6, author's paraphrase). "I know that the Lord maintains the cause of the afflicted and executes justice for the needy" (Ps. 140:12, author's paraphrase).

> God champions the cause of the oppressed and gives food to the hungry. The Lord sets the prisoners free and gives sight to the blind; the Lord lifts up those who are bowed down and loves the righteous. The Lord watches over the alien and sustains the fatherless and the widow, but he frustrates the ways of the wicked. (Ps. 146:7-8, author's paraphrase)

God works for justice. God also commands God's people to work for justice. "Justice, and only justice, you must follow, that your may live and inherit the land the Lord your God gives you" (Deut. 16:20, author's paraphrase).

> You shall not pervert the justice due to the foreigner or to the fatherless or take a widow's garment in pledge. But you shall remember that you were slaves in Egypt and the Lord

your God redeemed you from there. Therefore, I command you to maintain justice. (Deut. 24:17-18, author's paraphrase)

Wash and make yourselves clean. Take your evil deeds out of my sight! Stop doing wrong, learn to do right! Seek justice, [reprove the oppressor] encourage the oppressed. Defend the cause of the fatherless, plead the case of the widow." (Isa. 1:16-17, NIV)

"Thus says the Lord: preserve justice, and do righteousness" (Isa. 56:1, NASB). "Execute justice in the morning and rescue from the hand of his oppressor the one who has been robbed, or my wrath will break out and burn like fire because of your evil" (Jer. 21:12, author's paraphrase). "Break from your sins by doing justice and from your iniquities by showing mercy to the poor" (Dan. 4:27, author's paraphrase).

Doing social justice is more important to God than religious ritual and worship. "To do righteousness and justice is better to the Lord than sacrifice" (Prov. 21:3, author's paraphrase).

If you do away with the yoke of oppression, with the pointing finger and malicious talk, and if you spend yourselves on behalf of the hungry and satisfy the needs of the oppressed, then your light will rise in the darkness, and your night will become like the noonday. (Isa. 58:9b-10, NIV)

He has told you, O man, what is good. And what does the Lord require of you? To do justice, to love mercy, and to walk humbly with your God. (Micah 6:8, author's paraphrase)

You who turn justice into bitterness and cast righteousness to the ground . . . you hate the one who reproves in court and despise him to tells the truth. You trample on the poor

and force him to give you grain. Therefore, though you
have built stone mansions, you will not live in them. . . .
You oppress the righteous and take bribes and you deprive
the poor of justice. . . . I hate, I despise your religious feasts;
I cannot stand your assemblies. Even though you bring me
burnt offerings and grain offerings, I will not accept
them. . . . But let justice roll down like a river, and righteousness like a never-failing stream. (Amos 5:7, 10-12, 21-
22, 24, NIV; also see Jer. 7:4-7)

Jeremiah actually states that the knowledge of God and
doing justice are inseparable, that to know God *is* to do
justice.

Do you think you are a king simply because you have more
and more cedar? Did not your father have food and drink?
He established justice and righteousness, so all was well
with him. He championed the cause of the poor and the
needy, then it was well. *Is that not what it means to know me?*
declares the Lord. (22:15-16, author's paraphrase, emphasis
added)

Because God so loves social justice, God condemns
people and nations who neglect justice and condemns
people who benefit from injustice.

Surely the arm of the Lord is not too short to save, nor his
ear too dull to hear. But your iniquities have separated you
from your God; your sins have hidden his face from you, so
that he will not hear. . . . So justice is far from us and righteousness does not reach us. . . . We look for justice, but
find none. . . . Justice is driven back, and righteousness
stands at a distance. . . . The Lord looked and was dis-
pleased that there was no justice. He saw that there was no
one, he was appalled that there was no one to intervene.
(Isa. 59:1-2, 9, 11, 14, 16)

Sodom was destroyed by fire and brimstone because of its sexual wickedness, but also because of social injustice. "Now this was the sin of your sister Sodom: she and her daughters were arrogant, had abundant food and careless ease, but she did not help the poor and needy. . . . Therefore, I did away with them when I saw it" (Ezek. 16:49-50, author's paraphrase).

One major cause of the destruction and captivity of Israel was their failure to establish social justice. "They trample on the heads of the poor as upon the dust of the ground and deny justice to the oppressed. . . . Now then, I will crush you as a cart crushes when loaded with grain (Amos 2:7, 13, NIV).

> Hear this word, you cows of Bashan on Mt. Samaria, you women who oppress the poor and crush the needy and say to your husbands, 'Bring us something to drink!' The Sovereign Lord has sworn by his holiness: 'The time will come when you will be. . . . cast out, O mountain of oppression. (Amos 4:1-3, author's paraphrase)

God has a special love for the victims of injustice, for the poor, the hungry, the widow, the orphan, the foreigner, the little and vulnerable ones of the world. God identifies with them, hears their cries, and defends them. "You hear, O Lord, the desire of the afflicted; you encourage them and listen to their cry, defending the fatherless and the oppressed, in order that earthly humans may terrify no more" (Ps. 10:17-18, author's paraphrase). "Who is like you, O Lord? You rescue the poor from those too strong for them, the poor and needy from those who rob them" (Ps. 35:10, NIV). "Father of the fatherless and protector of widows is God in his holy habitation. God gives the desolate a home to dwell in; he leads out the prisoners to prosperity" (Ps. 68:5-6, RSV).

More than forty such passages command justice for orphans, widows, and foreigners. God so closely identifies himself with the poor as to actually become one of them. "He who oppresses a poor [person] insults his Maker" (Prov. 14:31, RSV). "He who is kind to the poor lends to the Lord" (Prov. 19:17, NIV). Jesus so identified with the poor and vulnerable that he could say, "I tell you the truth, whatever you did for one of the least of these brothers of mine, you did for me" (Matt. 25:40, NIV).

Justice for What?

But [al] justice is Christian business. But Christians so often fail to see this. One reason is that English translations of the Bible often obscure God's call for justice. The biblical words for justice in Hebrew (*mišpat, tsedaqah*) and in Greek (*dikaiosynē, krima, krisis*) are rich in meaning. They convey a sense of justice, righteousness, and judgment all at once.

But the English language doesn't have a single word that conveys these rich meanings, so the original is usually translated simply as *righteousness*. Unfortunately, many Christians misunderstand *righteousness* simply to mean individual piety. Thus God's passion for justice gets lost in translation. And Christians fail to realize how close to God's heart social justice is.

Why is social justice such a concern to God? To answer this, we need to first step back and ask a bigger question. What is God's project on earth?

God's project in this world is to establish a covenant relationship with people in history for the flourishing of human life in society. God wants human social life on earth to thrive. God wants people to live in communities of peace, prosperity, equity, and delightful relationships. To achieve this, God establishes covenant relationships with people (Adam and Eve, Noah, Abraham, the Israelites, and Christians). Within these relationships human social life can flourish. God always promises that faithfulness to the covenant brings *shalōm*. It bring peace, prosperity, equity, and enjoyable relationships.

So why does God have a passion for justice? Why is the struggle for social justice so central to the gospel of the kingdom? Because injustice violates God's project. It defiles the covenant and destroys shalom with poverty, greed, exploitation, oppression, and hunger. God is committed to achieving God's project in history through the church. God refuses to have God's righteous will violated by human sin. So, injustice must be opposed and destroyed.

Doing biblical justice, therefore, means *taking positive actions that create and preserve flourishing human community in fidelity to God's covenant.* This is why justice and righteousness are so closely linked in the mind of the Bible. To be righteous is to live in fidelity to the covenant, which is to realize a just social order.

This is also why justice, salvation, mercy, and love are all so closely connected in the Bible. To establish the justice of shalom in a sinful world is an act of salvation that requires mercy and love. To put it another way, God's merciful salvation necessarily results in social justice. (Thus, although many philosophers view love and justice as contradictory opposites, biblically speaking love and justice work and belong together.)

Sometimes people think of justice as retributive. They see it as negative, reactive, and punishment-oriented. Justice, they think, means judging and punishing wrongdoers. Likewise, sometimes people think of justice as procedural. It requires fair processes to resolve problems (such as the right to have one's contracts fulfilled, the right to a fair defense in court, and so on).

Justice in the Bible sometimes refers to retributive or procedural meanings of justice (e.g., Jer. 30:11; Deut.

16:19). But such meanings are not the dominant concerns of social justice in the Bible.

Biblical justice is more typically positive and distributive. It is primarily benefits-oriented, interested in undoing gross social inequalities. Biblical justice is concerned than no one be excluded from the benefits of society. It insists that every person have access to the minimum requirements necessary to participate in and contribute to society.

Hence biblical justice is especially concerned for the marginal members of society, those least able to take care of themselves, who would otherwise be excluded. This fits with the messianic description of the righteous king who champions the cause of the vulnerable, whose lives are precious.

> Endow the king with your justice, O God, the royal son with your righteousness. He will judge your people in righteousness, your afflicted ones with justice. . . . He will defend the afflicted among the people and save the children of the needy; he will crush the oppressor. . . . He will deliver the needy who cry out, the afflicted who have no one to help. He will take pity on the weak and needy and save the needy from death. He will rescue them from oppression and violence, for precious is their blood in his sight. (Ps. 72:1-2, 4, 12-14)

Justice Requires Institutional Change

When we talk about struggling for social justice, we are talking about social-structural change, political change, institutional change. To really grasp the issue at stake, we must explore the nature and dynamics of institutions.

Institutions are structures which people create to insure that what they want to happen will continue to happen, even long after they are dead and gone. Systems of government, law, education, finance, medicine, communication, transportation, and even religion are all institutions.

For example, the writers of the American constitution created an institution to try to insure that a relatively free society would exist for decades to come. People today create religious denominations as institutions to try to insure that future generations will continue to believe and worship in the time-honored ways.

Institutions have positive and negative sides. The positive side is that they foster stability and continuity. Because of our electoral institutions, we don't need repeatedly to decide how to choose our next President. We already know that because those decisions have been institutionalized, and we are faced only with the easier problem of deciding whom to elect.

The negative side of institutions is twofold. First, institutions produce emergent effects. These are unintended social consequences. Emergent effects can be negative, even evil, but they do not necessarily reflect the intentions of the individuals involved. God pointed this out, for example, in saying that the establishment of a monarchical state in Israel would lead to oppression and injustice in the land (1 Sam. 8:9-18).

Our complex modern world is full of emergent effects. The emergent effect of a stock-market panic (everyone selling at once) is a stock-market crash. No one intends it. It just happens. An emergent effect of a car accident on the other side of a highway, when everyone slows down to look, is a traffic jam. No one intends or wants it to happen; it just does. An emergent effect of Third World countries trying to boost their gross national product by growing and exporting a single, cash crop is that peasants go hungry because beans and corn are not grown for local consumption. The intent is to improve economic conditions; the emergent effect is to worsen them.

The second negative side of institutions is that they are hard to change. This is by design. The harder an institution is to change, the more certain the people who designed it can be that what they want to happen will continue to happen. In this sense, institutions have a life of their own, a self-perpetuating inertia and autonomy. It's as if they are set on an automatic pilot directing their behavior indefinitely.

Institutions should be, and usually are, designed to promote human well-being. But institutions often turn out to harm the common good. Sometimes the people that started the institution were wrong in their motives or objectives. Sometimes the institutions gradually lose their direction or purpose. Sometimes institutions themselves remain the same but the world around them changes, rendering them irrelevant or harmful. In any case, institutions can come to hurt, rather than promote, human well-being. When that happens God's will is violated and those institutions need to be changed.

Understanding institutions helps us see why political, social-structural change is necessary. First, the world will not automatically change if enough individuals change, because society is more than the sum total of all living individuals. Society also includes all the self-perpetuating institutions which people have created over hundreds of years. Any number of individuals can be changed, but that, in itself, won't change society. Institutions were created structurally and must be changed structurally.

Second, a right understanding of institutions tells us personal change cannot be divorced from institutional change. Why? Just as people are makers of institutions, institutions are makers of people. This is sometimes hard to accept, for our individualism teaches us we are autonomous and self-made, not shaped by society.

But the myths of Robinson Crusoe and the Lone Ranger

are just that—myths. No one lives in a social vacuum or stands above the power of institutions and culture. Our very existence and identity as individuals presupposes the social institutions of family, language, education, material production, legal order, and so on. Without denying individual relative-freedom and responsibility, we must recognize that our moral and spiritual experience is significantly shaped by the larger social world.

For example, the rates for drunkenness, spouse abuse, child abuse, divorce, and suicide increase remarkably when unemployment increases. This does not show that newly unemployed people suddenly become morally and spiritually inferior to the still-employed. It shows that people in economically depressed areas make moral choices in a social context which often fails to support right moral behavior. Clearly the social setting of unemployment does not excuse personal responsibility for one's actions. But neither does personal responsibility negate the shaping power of social context.

Some Christians argue that since the root of all social evil is the human heart, social evil will persist until all human hearts are purified. There may be truth here. But it does not offer a valid argument against Christian social action for several reasons.

First, people bear God's image and are not purely evil. People are capable of good as well evil. And as we've just seen, human moral actions are shaped in part by the context in which the actions take place. One goal of structural transformation is to create a social world which better encourages and rewards individual righteousness. This principle seems to have guided both Paul and Peter (Rom. 13:3-4; 1 Pet. 2:14).

Second, institutions are not necessarily direct reflections of the sin in contemporary peoples' hearts. They may reflect the evil hearts of people long dead. Institutions can indeed nurture and protect evil. They can be used by evil people for evil ends. But many institutions reflect the human impulse for good, to preserve human life and enrich it. Institutions can nurture righteousness and facilitate good for the people whose lives they touch.

Third, because of the self-perpetuating autonomy of institutions and the reality of emergent effects, any institution may accomplish injustice as an unintended consequence. Institutional sin is often an unintended emergent effect, not directly traceable to individual sins. System-wide changes are necessary, then, to alter the structures which give rise to unintended emergent effects.

Fourth, if the hearts of Christians have been changed, then why shouldn't those who have experienced spiritual renewal work for social-structural transformation leading to justice? Why wait for 100 percent spiritual renewal before promoting a just world? The Bible itself teaches that the gospel—as the church in the world becomes salt, yeast, and light—works for the good of the whole society (Matt. 5:13-16; Luke 13:20-21).

But Is Social Change Really Possible?

Many Christians decline the struggle for justice because they say justice will never be realized until Jesus returns and we go to heaven bye and bye. In the meantime, they say, we have to live with the world as it is.

Besides conveniently rationalizing the thoughtless indulgence of middle-class comforts, this theology mistakenly relegates God's kingdom to the distant future. It disconnects God's kingdom from history. This distorts the good news, making it good news only for those whose lives are already quite nice.

Middle-class North American Christians often ignore the call for justice because they do not themselves suffer from social injustices. Social problems seem less urgent when they don't damage one's life. Middle-class people will have little incentive to work for social-structural change if they see the social system as benign and project that view onto the entire world.

But to excuse ourselves from the struggle for social justice simply because we don't happen to be the present victims of injustice is ungodly. It is to deny the call of God on those who would follow Jesus.

I suspect, however, that these are not the most important reasons Christians often ignore justice. The deepest reason may be that deep down many Christians don't think social change is possible. People can't bear knowing that something must be done that (they think) can't be done. So they convince themselves that social change need not be attempted.

Institutions, we have seen, are by nature difficult to change. The institutions of modern, industrialized societies are more so, because they are not just institutions. They are mega-institutions. Think about them—national government bureaucracies, the federal legal system, international banking, multinational corporations, the military-industrial complex, television networks, the medical industry.

They have grown enormously in size and complexity. This makes them seem utterly inaccessible, beyond the reach of any individual, beyond the forces of change. How, we ask ourselves, can we change society when we can't even get the local police station to cancel a parking ticket we didn't deserve?

In the face of apparently inaccessible and immobile mega-institutions, many people resign themselves to defensively coexisting with them. They try to maximize the personal benefits and minimize the personal losses of life in the modern world. Instead of engaging in the struggle for justice in the public world, *their* public world, they re-treat into the less intimidating, more manageable private world. Seemingly cut off from the possibility of making an impact on society, they withdraw into the experience of nuclear family, close friends, personal career, self-fulfill-ment, leisure, and privatized religion.

The result is deep alienation from one's own society and a feeling of defenselessness and dependence before an overwhelming system. Beneath the personal accomplish-ments and enjoyments of privatized life, a deep dis-ease, the awareness of social powerlessness and vulnerability, gnaws.

But if it is true that the church really can't change soci-ety, that we can't do justice, it is only so because we make it true by believing it. Society is, after all, nothing more than the interrelated system of institutions created by people in past and present years. If humanly created, they can be hu-manly re-created.

The key is getting focused. It is realizing that while the whole world can't be changed, pieces of the world can change. Specific situations of injustice can be transformed. New institutions can be brought into existence. The whole world is overwhelming. But a specific issue or problem is not. We need to target our efforts.

We can't solve the problem of world hunger. But we can work on specific trade or aid laws, entrepreneurial busi-ness projects in a Third-World city, or policy reforms in a specific multinational corporation. We can't end family problems. But we can rewrite divorce laws, institute shel-ters for abused children and spouses, or work on child-support policies. We need to change what we can, howev-er modest that may be, rather than complaining that since we can't change everything we might as well not change anything.

Christians possess no lack of resources. There are, for

example, 130 million active Christians in North America. We represent many billions of dollars of annual earning and spending power. Christians have demonstrated keen skill in political organizing. We control a massive network of educational, publishing, and communications institutions. Furthermore, Christians possess a faith-motivated orientation to life which can transcend the neutralizing effect of self-interested living. We bring all this to a multilevel political system which is not entirely unresponsive to the demands of its citizens, an economic system which allows new business start-ups, and a cultural-legal system which allows for the creation of new social institutions.

On what basis do we then claim that we are helpless to bring about any meaningful social changes? Our helplessness is in our minds. If we have not been successful in our struggles for social justice, it is not because it can never be done or because God is uninterested. One key reason may be that we have not adequately developed the conviction, the knowledge, and the organizations to do it.

Where Christians *have* organized to work for justice, they have often made significant changes. Nineteenth-century Christian abolitionists, for example, helped eradicate slavery, a deeply rooted injustice as old as human record. Turn-of-the-century believers were key in the movement to found orphanages and homes for the destitute. For years, Christians led the fight against apartheid in South Africa, which is now showing signs of promise.

In the 1980s, Christians working to oppose the U.S.-sponsored war in Central America succeeded in preventing a more direct U.S. invasion of Nicaragua. And today in Latin America, ordinary Christians, organized in grassroots base ecclesial communities, are struggling for liberation and participatory democracy. At a 1987 meeting of base communities in Santiago, Chile, one gray-haired man assured me, his voice steady with dignity and determination, "We will get rid of our brutal dictator, Augusto Pinochet, by Christmas, I promise." Pinochet was ousted from the presidency by vote within a year.

Where to Begin

Once we see and accept that the struggle for social justice is Christian business, a necessary part of church renewal, what do we do next? Where do we go from there?

The natural tendency is toward immediate action. We ask, "What can I *do now* against injustice?" That is natural. It is also a mistake.

Before we can change anything, we must first be changed, deeply changed. Here we see that there is some truth in the notion that social change starts with the human heart. We as churches need to become converted to God's passion for social justice. We need simply to sit still and let the fact that God loves and works for justice, and calls us to the same, sink into our souls, minds, hearts, emotions.

It's not that (as conformist theologies tell us) *everyone* must change before anything can change. It's simply that *we* first need to be changed. We need to repent of indifference to the cause of justice. We have to change our thoughts, feelings, desires, and identity so that the concern for justice becomes a natural part of our consciousness. We must learn to see life from the perspective of the vulnerable, the abused, the marginalized. We have to allow ourselves to feel the suffering and anger of those who suffer unjustly. And we need to set our deepest longings on God's final day of complete justice.

We must be honest here. Being converted to the struggle for justice means voluntarily choosing to make our lives more difficult. It means taking on yet more burdens, more concerns, and more suffering. Why would anyone do that? Because these are God's burdens, because God chooses to suffer with the victims of injustice, and because God calls us to the same. Are not Christians called to suffer and struggle (Rom. 5:3-4; 2 Tim. 1:8; 1 Pet. 2:20-21)?

If we are not first changed, if we are not deeply converted, then our initial flurry of justice-activism will soon be overwhelmed by busy schedules and discouragement. The struggle for justice is not easy. If the struggle is not truly part of our basic identities, truly a lifelong commitment, we will soon give up and rationalize away God's call for justice. So personal and collective conversion must come first.

But once we are changing and becoming converted, what then? Again, immediate action does not come next. Next we need to make our church communities places of justice—of peace, equity, and delightful relationships. The church is the outpost of the reign of God, the demonstration project of God's kingdom. Thus social justice must begin with the church.

After that, before jumping into activism, we as churches must *become educated*. To struggle for justice, we need to learn about the causes of injustice. We have to study history, sociology, politics, law, and economics to learn about the way the world works, how it ticks. We must also learn about how injustice has been and can be challenged. Becoming educated is hard work. There are no shortcuts. But without the tools of social analysis and understanding, our struggle for justice will be ineffective.

Only after we've been converted and we've started to educate ourselves should we become active. Only then is it time to invest ourselves directly in the struggle for social justice. Of course, activism itself will be educational. From it we will learn things about the world we never knew (and might not have wanted to know!).

Once we've become active, the possibilities are endless.

There are many injustices to be challenged. And there are many worthy organizations and movements—Christian and secular—to plug into. Bread for the World, Witness for Peace, the Mennonite Central Committee, Amnesty International, Oxfam, World Vision, Habitat for Humanity, and Evangelicals for Social Action are just a few.

We can join or start a local chapter of an existing organization, or we can found an entirely new group. We can work on a single issue, such as the problem of the homeless, or an array of related issues, such as poverty and militarism in the Third World. We can organize locally, regionally, or nationally. What to do depends on how God is calling us and what makes the most sense, given our particular interests, resources, and situations.

God loves justice and is working to change human history, to turn this sinful world around, to bring in the kingdom, to make "all things new" (Rev. 21:5, NASB). Jesus confronts us with the call to repent—to change the direction of our lives (Mark 1:15; Rom. 12:2). When we become Christians, we throw in our lives with a divine movement toward "a new creation" (Gal. 6:15, NIV), "a new heaven and a new earth" (2 Pet. 3:13; Rev. 21:1, NIV), "a new human" (2 Cor. 5:17; Eph. 4:24; Col. 3:10, NIV), and a "new Jerusalem" (Rev. 21:2, NIV).

Clearly change is at the heart of our faith. And nothing in all of creation will escape God's passionate work for justice and redemptive change. If we want our churches to be alive and well, we had better join God in the struggle for social justice.

9

Do Grass-Roots Ecumenism

RADICAL CHURCH RENEWAL rejects the unnecessary divisions that separate and isolate Christians from each other. It calls believers to work for unity in the Spirit. But to be meaningful and effective, this work must become the bottom-up, grass-roots work of the people of God.

Called to Unity
God calls Christians to unity. The core meaning of the gospel itself is that by grace the wall that separates us from God is broken down. So is every wall that alienates us from each other (Eph. 2:11-22; Col. 3:11; 1 Cor. 12:13). All the barriers that usually divide people—religious traditions and rituals, race, gender, social status—can no longer separate believers in Jesus (Gal. 3:28).

Unity is a gift from the hand of God (2 Chron. 30:12; Jer 32:39). In the church, God gives the gifts of the Spirit, "so that the body of Christ may be built up until we all reach *unity* in the faith and in the knowledge of the Son of God" (Eph. 4:11-13, NIV).

The apostle Paul earnestly desired unity in the church. "May the God who gives endurance and encouragement give you *a spirit of unity* . . . so that with one heart and mouth you may glorify the God and Father of our Lord Jesus Christ" (Rom. 15:5-6, NIV).

Paul rebuked believers for disunity (1 Cor. 11:18) and commanded believers to struggle for unity. "Make every effort to keep the *unity of the Spirit* through the bond of peace" (Eph. 4:3, NIV). According to Paul, the church should live as one because God and our faith are one. "There is one body and one Spirit . . . one hope . . . one Lord, one faith, one baptism, one God and Father of all" (Eph. 4:4, NIV).

Jesus himself, in his last words to his disciples, clearly declared that the unity of Christian believers would be a witness that Christ was sent from God.

> I pray . . . that all of them may be one, Father, just as you are in me and I am in you. May they also be in us so that the world may believe that you have sent me. . . . May they be brought to complete unity to let the world know that you sent me. (John 17:20-21, 23, NIV)

This unity was demonstrated in the first church where "all the believers were one in heart and mind" (Acts 4:32, NIV; also see Acts 2:42-47). What was the result of this unity? "The Lord added to their number daily those who were being saved" (Acts 2:47, NIV).

A skeptic might argue that these passages only call for internal unity within individual congregations, not unity among Christians in general. But that counters the thrust of the entire New Testament. Furthermore, even the churches at Antioch and Jerusalem, located hundreds of miles apart, worked hard to resolve a matter of sharp dispute (Acts 15). Paul also constantly·encouraged relationships of love and unity between believers from different churches (Rom. 16:1-2; 1 Cor. 16:19; Eph. 6:21-22; Phil. 4:22; Col. 4:7-15; 2 Tim. 4:19-21; Titus 3:13-15; Philem. 23; also see 1 Pet. 5:13).

Thus from the Old Testament, where the psalmist declares "How good and pleasant it is when brothers live together in unity" (Ps. 133:1, NIV), to the New Testament, where believers are called to "stand firm in one spirit" (Phil. 1:27, NIV) we see that God wants God's people to live in unity.

The Scandal of Division

But Christians today do not live in unity. Contemporary Christianity is characterized by deep schisms in spirit and structure.

The church today is divided into more than 150 organized traditions and denominations. In the United States, there are thirteen Baptist denominations alone. In North America, churches have been rent over all sorts of social, theological, cultural, ecclesiastical, and political issues.

Some denominations split more than a century ago over slavery. Other affluent denominations split to protect the economic status of their wealthy members from the incursion of lower-class Christians. Other sects formed to preserve their Finnish, Polish, German, Russian, Armenian, or other ethnic identities.

Some denominations split in protest against the informality and emotionalism of frontier revivalists. Some Christian groups have even separated over whether to have musical instruments in church or whether using buttons is sinful (though the concern for simplicity lying behind the Amish opposition to buttons deserves respect).

Not only that, churches often construct their identities at the expense of other Christians around them. Churches frequently establish themselves by tearing others down. They strengthen their in-group feeling by creating and attacking out-groups. Denominations or adherents of entire theological traditions also do this. You can see it and hear it everywhere, sometimes over the most trivial issues.

Protestants openly tear down Catholics. Free-will Arminians arrogantly ridicule Calvinists. Informal churches smugly mock high liturgy churches (a sin proponents of radical church renewal must beware of!). Traditionalists publicly scorn charismatics. And vice versa.

"How can a Catholic be saved? They worship Mary! How ridiculous!" "Predestination! How stupid can you be to think that God decides who to save and who to damn!" "Baptists deny the sovereignty of God. They don't even believe in infant baptism!" "All that stuffy, formal liturgy is meaningless! You can't worship God that way." "Speaking in tongues is totally unbiblical—weird, too!" "*Our* denomination believes in having the eucharist *every week*!"

Each faction believes it has the real and final truth. All others have misunderstood the Bible. Immeasurable amounts of time, energy, and money are spent to prove and separate who is wrong and who is right. Sermons are preached. Seminaries are built. Tracts are written. Children are instructed. The hard boundaries between Christians are carefully drawn. And they are not often crossed.

In this way, the church becomes a dysfunctional family. Brothers and sisters incessantly feud, form cliques, tear each other down, refuse to speak. The question is, who would ever want to become an adopted member of this kind of family?

Such divisions are a scandal. The disunity is an anti-gospel witness. Unbelievers cannot look at the churches and say, "Now there is a power reconciling people to live in love and unity." What they *can* say is, "The church looks and acts just like any other organization, so what's the big deal?" H. Richard Niebuhr was more than a little right in claiming that denominationalism represented Christianity's moral failure.

If we are serious about renewing the church, this situation must change.

Unity, Not Uniformity, Not Relativism

It is important to understand what the goal of grass-roots ecumenism is and is not. The Bible calls the church to unity, not uniformity. Unity means oneness, a harmony of diversity. Uniformity means sameness, an absence of diversity.

God wants unity. But unlike fascist dictators and fast-food production managers, God is no fan of uniformity. One look at the universe God created, with all its variations, contrasts, idiosyncrasies, and colors, tells us God dislikes uniformity.

The purpose of ecumenism is not to force all Christians to look, think, act, and believe alike. It is not to obliterate all variations. Because of diverse traditions, cultural heritages, national histories, and group personalities, Christians will always be different from each other. Many differences are valid. It is often good for churches to recognize, appreciate, and celebrate their unique characteristics. So uniformity is not the goal.

Neither is relativism the goal. Some people take a short-cut to Christian unity by abandoning truth and conviction altogether. They say, in effect, "Whatever you believe is okay, if it's good for you. One doctrine is as good as the next. I just accept whatever anyone is into." Here are people whose minds are so open their brains fall out.

Grass-roots ecumenism does not ignore the question of

truth. Nor does it abandon theological convictions or rela-
tivize all religious beliefs. It does not put an end to theological discussions by sweeping disagreements under the
rug. Rather than denying or downplaying differences in
theological convictions, grass-roots ecumenism recognizes differences. It then responds to them in a way that nur-
tures rather than destroys unity in the body of Christ.

Grass-roots ecumenism actually revels in vigorous
theological challenge and interchange. But it addresses
differences with a style and tone that reflects a genuine
openness, mutuality, and respect among the participants.
In grass-roots ecumenism, the primary goal of the discussion is not to refute and conquer one's doctrinal opponent.
It is instead to stretch people's theological understandings
so they grow in Christian wisdom and knowledge. The
goal is to learn from and be enriched by each other and to
work toward common theological ground. Only having
begun with mutual openness and respect can we correct
each other's theological weaknesses and faults.

Sorting Out Different Types of Differences

A key cause of disunity among Christians is that many
churches and denominations think *their* issues are *the* issues allowing no compromise. Grass-roots ecumenism
thus calls for an ability to distinguish between types of
theological differences to determine what is really important and what is not.

At one end of the spectrum, some beliefs are essential to
the Christian faith. Differences here don't divide Christian
from Christian, but Christian from non-Christian. These
basic beliefs are fairly apparent, since the church spent
centuries identifying and clarifying them. They include the
Trinity, human sin, the deity of Christ, salvation by faith,
and so on. The Apostles' Creed, for example, summarizes

what is nonnegotiable in Christianity.

At the other end of the spectrum are theological differences that amount to nothing more than personal inclinations and stylistic preferences. Examples include whether to sing only psalms or hymns as well, whether to follow the Christian calender, whether to baptize by immersion or pouring, and whether daily devotional "quiet times" are essential to spiritual growth.

Some may insist these are critical matters of normative significance. But in the big scheme of things, they seem to border on the trivial and are not worth much time and energy spent on debate. Let us call these *preferences*.

Between these ends of the spectrum lie important beliefs over which Christians legitimately can and do disagree. Typically, these are matters that have been debated for centuries and probably will never be fully resolved in history. They include disputes over predestination, infant baptism, divorce, the Lord's Supper, the role of women, eschatology, the Sabbath, and so on. Let us call these *unresolved disputes*.

Unresolved disputes are not merely personal preferences. They are important matters which involve right and wrong. Hence they require commitment and deserve ongoing discussion (indeed, this book itself is an argument for a certain perspective on mostly these kinds of issues).

At the same time, unresolved disputes are not Christian essentials. They do not concern the basics of the faith. For this reason and because they appear historically irresolvable, Christians should not allow differences on these issues to tear them apart.

Division is justified over Christian essentials. Breaking relationships is justified over unrepented sin (1 Cor. 5:11-13). But while unresolved disputes are important, they are not important enough to violate unity in the body of Christ. Christians must simply agree to disagree on these matters and continue to be brothers and sisters in Christ.

Furthermore, grass-roots ecumenism recognizes that while theological differences are not unimportant, they are not all-important. Some Christians are such doctrinal legalists, so obsessed with right belief, that they neglect right action. But living a faithful Christian life does not consist of writing and defending the perfect systematic theology. We must remember that, according to Scripture, ortho*praxis* is as important as orthodoxy (Matt. 7:24-27). James, for example, emphasizes the importance of acting on what we profess to believe.

> Belief by itself, if it is not accompanied by action, is dead. But someone will say, "You have belief, I have deeds." Show me your belief without deeds, and I will show you my belief by what I do. . . . You see that a person is justified by what he does and not by belief alone. (James 2:17-18, 24, author's paraphrase; see also James 1:22-25)

In the end, grass-roots ecumenism grows out of a humility that comes from the realization that no one theology or tradition holds the fullness of truth. This no doubt includes this book's vision of radical church renewal. Each has strengths and weaknesses. Each may have interpreted the Bible rightly on some points and wrongly on others. Thus traditions can compliment each other and diversity can bring spiritual stability, strength, and stimulation instead of automatic conflict and division.

Consequently, we should not encourage fellowship only with people who think, believe, look, and act just like ourselves. Grass-roots ecumenism calls Christians to openly learn from and be challenged and strengthened by the diverse backgrounds of our different sisters and brothers in the faith. As eighteenth-century Methodist revivalist John Wesley exclaimed,

I refuse to be distinguished from other men by any but the common principles of Christianity. . . . I renounce and detest all other marks of distinction. But from real Christians, of whatever denomination, I earnestly desire not to be distinguished at all. . . . Dost thou love and fear God? It is enough! I give thee the right hand of fellowship.

From the Bottom Up

Christian unity is a key challenge for the church. But for too long unity has been left to elites. For the most part over the years, ecumenism has largely consisted of inter-denominational congresses for religious "dialogue" attended by church and denominational professionals. Position papers, declarations, and resolutions often emanate from these meetings, which may or may not eventually filter down to the laity.

I don't disparage these sorts of conferences and meetings. Many have been helpful. The World Missionary Conference of 1910 in Edinburgh, Scotland, was tremendously significant, as was the second assembly of the World Council of Churches in Evanston, Illinois, in 1954. Vatican II also was key in changing how Catholics deal with other Christians.

I think it is important, however, to acknowledge that while ecumenical conferences for church elites may be important and necessary, they are also inadequate. Top-down ecumenism entails major built-in constraints. Even some ecumenical leaders have recognized this.

The biggest constraint is caused by the gap between the clergy and the laity, that inevitable by-product of the clergy system. The gap inhibits top-down ecumenism from fully working its way down to the people in a way that meaningfully alters their experiences. Far-off conferences, which may excite church leaders, often mean little to the people in the pews.

That some church leaders even assume ecumenism can be implemented from above reflects an overestimation of the power of their own positions. The people of God, not ecclesiastical professionals, are the church. Authentic ecumenism is primarily the work of the people of God, not of church elites. Again, ecumenical leaders often have been among the first to recognize this.

Ecumenism with any chance of achieving real Christian unity will have to be grass-roots and bottom-up. It will have to be built not only on the formal resolutions of conferences but on real, personal *relationships* among ordinary people of God. In the end, it will only be dynamic networks of personal relationships that break down the theological and psychological walls that currently isolate and separate Christian from Christian.

Two Strategic Goals

Grass-roots ecumenism has two major strategic goals. A first and more modest goal is straightforward and could be accomplished in a matter of years. The goal is to have ordinary Christians from different traditions and denominations get to know and talk with each other. It is for all believers to step out from behind their carefully erected and defended theological and organizational walls to meet and listen to each other. We could thus learn better to understand and appreciate each other.

As a first step, this requires that Christians stop tearing each other down, especially in public, for their differences. Rather than building themselves up by attacking outsiders, each church and denomination must start humbly to examine itself for its own weaknesses or sins (Matt. 7:1-5).

After that, one way for a church in renewal to get started is for members to get together with those of another church from a different tradition simply to talk and learn from each other. This can involve two families sharing or entire congregations going on weekend retreats together. The point is to establish contacts with Christians from different backgrounds, to get to know them, to discover how they understand their faith and how that shapes and enriches their lives.

Another means is through local theological cross-pollenization. My church, for example, does something we call "Theology Workshop," where a group of us read and discuss important theological works. Over the years we have read Luther's *Lectures on Galatians*, Calvin's *Institutes*, the Catholic Bishop's *Pastoral Letter on the Economy*, sections of Barth's *Dogmatics*, Smede's evangelical *Sex for Christians*, Augustine's *Confessions*, Kraybill's *The Upside-Down Kingdom*, and much more.

The cross-fertilization of so many traditions has enriched our spirits and profoundly shaped our community's spirituality. It probably would have been even more enriching to invite someone from the theological tradition we were studying to discuss the book with us.

Perhaps the most effective way to help achieve the first, modest goal is to work together with diverse believers on service and social justice projects. Doing so automatically shifts the focus from arguing over disagreements to accomplishing commonly shared goals. Quarrels over infant versus adult baptism, for example, become irrelevant when there are two hundred hungry, homeless people lined up at the shelter for a meal.

By working closely with believers from other traditions, we realize they often don't fit our stereotypes. Once our discomfort with "the other" begins to recede, we can appreciate how much we do share in common. Heretofore "heterodox" strangers gradually become friends and partners. Eventually we realize how much we appreciate, have learned from, and need them.

In working together with different sorts of Christians in service and social justice projects, differences in doctrine or ethics will come up. But when they do, they can be addressed in the context of a working partnership of allies trying to express themselves and understand each other. This is more fruitful than having divided strangers heave theological rocks at each other.

Recently a conservative Protestant friend told me how surprised he was to discover, at age fifty-five, what Roman Catholics were actually like. He *thought* Catholics were all rule-driven, ritual-ridden, saint-worshipers. Then he began to work with some Catholics on a local political election campaign.

His stereotypes burst. These Catholics, he discovered, basically loved the Lord and wanted to follow God as best they knew how. "Some of them," he reported with amazed fondness, "can out-'Praise-the-Lord!' any Christians I've met."

Yet another way grass-roots unity can be built is through forming ecumenical Christian church communities. Such ecumenical communities draw together believers from all backgrounds and unite them in relationships of commitment, trust, and love. These communities model Christian unity at a personal level. Churches in the process of radical renewal might decide, while maintaining roots in their basic traditions, to declare themselves ecumenical and open to believers of different stripes.

The goal of having Christians from different perspectives get to know each other is to effect real change in Christians' attitudes toward those on different sides of disputes. Achieving this will be a major accomplishment.

This widespread personal change at the grass-roots level will then lay the foundation for a second, less modest goal of grass-roots ecumenism. That goal is structural change at the denominational level.

In the end it is not enough to establish unity only at a personal level, however fundamental that is. It is necessary to establish greater unity at a structural level. This will mean dismantling some church structures that divide.

Christians who have reached across divisions at the personal level should be able to tear down denominational structures of division. This will include merging denominations and conferences within similar confessional traditions. The guiding principle should be to merge the easier cases first, then tackle more difficult cases.

Many examples of this structural "de-fragmentation" already exist and can serve as models for future unification. In 1918, three Lutheran synods merged as the United Lutheran Church. In 1939, three Methodist denominations united to form the Methodist Church. In 1957, four denominations combined to form the United Church of Christ. In 1958, the United Presbyterian Church joined with the Presbyterian Church (U.S.A.). Today the General Conference Mennonite Church and the Mennonite Church are seriously considering merger. More such unions can and should occur. Would it not be desirable to have simply one or two associations or confederations of churches representing, for example, the Anabaptist, Reformed, Lutheran, Wesleyan, and Episcopal churches?

Building meaningful structural unity, however, will require more than simply merging organizations and shuffling denominational names around. It will also require a basic change in denominational self-understandings. Denominations will have to redefine themselves in terms of their function and mission.

Instead of each denomination viewing itself as the faithful defender of the true version of the faith, each will have to come to see itself simply as the institutional carrier of one valuable, but limited, Christian tradition. This will require a non-triumphalist self-confidence allowing greater openness, humility, and self-criticism.

It will also require a more realistic sense of a tradition's strengths and limitations. The key task here will be to maintain the rich variety of Christian confessional traditions without fragmenting the traditions or having them resort to antagonistic competition and mutual attacks.

It appears that in heaven there will be no organized denominations. All of Jesus' different disciples will be united as one in praise and obedience to God (Rev. 21). As our history is drawn into that inevitable future, should not the lives of our churches at least partially reflect that destiny? Even in this sinful, broken world, might it not be possible for this and the next generation of Christians in search of renewal to turn the more than 150 denominations into a handful of denominations? Even that might be a compromise. Still it would be a God glorifying achievement of major proportions.

Local churches on the road to radical renewal need to take the scandal of fragmentation and division seriously. In creative response, they must work at all levels to restore greater unity to the body of Christ.

CONCLUSION

Pioneers of a New Paradigm

THIS BOOK has advanced nine proposals that together point to an overarching vision for renewal that goes to our roots in the Bible and the early church under the Spirit's guidance. This vision of radical church renewal is grounded in the growing worldwide movement to transform the church from the bottom up.

The radical vision presented here is *not* radical in the sense that it is utopian or outlandish. Indeed, the vision grows from the real, lived experience of the author and millions of other believers in alternative churches around the world. Many of the proposals, though radical to many people today, are quite traditional in that they reflect practices of the first churches. In this sense, many features of the so-called "traditional" church are not traditional at all. They are historical deviations from the original vision.

What *is* radical about radical church renewal is that it tries to deals with the *roots* of the church's problems. The word *radical* means "to the roots." Hence the vision of church renewal presented here tries to dig down to the bottom of the church's ailments. It aims to prescribe changes profound enough to bring a real newness of life to churches.

An Ecclesiological Paradigm Shift

In scientific language, radical church renewal requires a genuine *paradigm shift* in our understanding of church.

A *paradigm*—a term popularized by philosopher of science, Thomas Kuhn—is an overarching framework of understanding. It is a particular model for understanding, a certain lens through which to look in interpreting data. A paradigm tells you what assumptions to make and what questions to ask. It guides you toward evidence relevant to the paradigm's understanding of the world. The workings of a paradigm tend only to make sense within the paradigm itself.

A paradigm shift occurs when one paradigm is rejected and new one embraced. A paradigm shift involves adopting an entirely different set of assumptions and questions through which to make sense of reality. Why do paradigm shifts occur? Because people perceive that their old paradigm is increasingly unable to interpret the world and an emerging paradigm promises to do a better job.

For example, for centuries Western astronomers worked with a geocentric paradigm of the universe. They believed the planets revolved around the earth. That paradigm informed the assumptions they made, the questions they asked, and the data they believed was relevant. The geocentric paradigm worked for a while. But with time, it increasingly failed correctly to explain the movements of the planets.

Eventually an iconoclast named Copernicus proposed a new, heliocentric paradigm of the universe. He argued that the planets actually revolve around the sun. That was a radical shift in thinking. Few astronomers accepted it at first. Eventually, however, astronomers adopted the heliocentric paradigm because they saw that it did make better sense of planet motion. This was one of astronomy's paradigm shifts.

What ultimately makes church renewal radical is that it is uninterested in merely correcting, adjusting, or improving the established church paradigm. It believes the old paradigm is fundamentally inadequate for making sense of Christianity in the world today. Instead, it calls for a genuine paradigm shift. It wants to replace the old framework of understanding the church with a very different one. This new paradigm will make a different set of assumptions, ask a different set of questions, hold a different set of expectations when it comes to church.

Pioneers of the Future

As in the days of Copernicus, many Christians are maintaining and defending the old church paradigm. They either believe it is sufficient itself or find the alternative church paradigm too unconventional to make the shift. Some have invested too much of their careers in the old church paradigm to abandon it now. That is all right. People will make the shift when they are ready.

But a growing number of Christians in North America and in other parts of the world *are* making a paradigm shift. They have discovered too many inadequacies in the old church paradigm.

Having tried the small-group movement, for example, they have concluded that small groups are not enough. Having tried the church-growth movement, they have determined that church-growth techniques are not enough. Having experienced charismatic gifts, they have decided that miraculous signs and wonders are not enough. Having fought long and hard to get their established churches to come to life, they have concluded that there is something intrinsically wrong with the established church itself. Some of them are searching. Some are desperate.

These are the people who will be the North American pioneers of radical church renewal. They are the ones who will innovate a new, more authentic and faithful experience of church in this culture. Naturally, each pioneering church must discover a path of radical renewal that is appropriate for its unique situation. But whatever form it takes, renewal must go to the roots.

These pioneers will cut new trails. They will build Christian community; reconstruct ministry as the work of all the people of God; decentralize leadership and decision making; actually implement the priesthood of all believers in worship; break free from the burden of church buildings; explore together a new spirituality of everyday life; practice lifestyle evangelism; struggle for social justice; and work for unity in the fractured body of Christ.

As the radical pioneers blaze these fresh trails, they will renew their own churches today and many more churches tomorrow.

For Further Reading

Christian Community

Bonhoeffer, Deitrich. *Life Together*, New York: Harper & Row, 1976.

Gish, Art. *Living in Christian Community*, Scottdale, Pa.: Herald Press, 1979.

Jackson, Dave. *Coming Together: All Those Communities and What They're Up To*, Bethany Fellowship, 1978.

Jackson, Dave and Neta. *Living Together in a World Falling Apart*, Altamonte Springs, Fla.: Creation House, 1974.

_____. *Glimpses of Glory: Thirty Years of Community*, Elgin, Ill.: Brethren Press, 1987.

O'Halloran, James. *Living Cells: Developing Small Christian Community*, Maryknoll, N.Y.: Orbis Books, 1984.

Snyder, Howard. *The Community of the King*, Downers Grove, Ill.: InterVarsity Press, 1977.

Wagemaker, Herbert. *The Christian Community: A Special Kind of Belonging*, Waco, Tex.: Word, 1978.

Whitehead, Evelyn & James. *Community of Faith: Models and Strategies for Developing Christian Communities*, San Francisco, Calif.: Seabury Press, 1982.

Christian Relationships

Augsburger, David. *Caring Enough to Confront*, Scottdale, Pa.: Herald Press, 1980.

_____. *Caring Enough to Forgive*, Scottdale, Pa.: Herald Press, 1981.

Jackson, Neta. *A New Way to Live*, Scottdale, Pa.: Herald Press, 1983.

O'Connor, Elizabeth. *The New Community*, New York: Harper & Row, 1976.

Smedes, Lewis. *Forgive and Forget: Healing the Hurts We Don't Deserve*, New York: Harper & Row, 1984.

_____. *Caring and Commitment: Learning to Live the Love We Promise*, New York: Harper & Row, 1988.

Vanier, Jean. *Community and Growth*, Mahwah, N.J.: Paulist Press, 1979.

Participatory Ministry, Leadership, and Decision Making

Avery, Michael. *Building United Judgments: A Handbook for Consensus Decision Making*, Madison, Wis.: Center for Conflict Resolution, 1981.

Banks, Robert. *Going to Church in the First Century*, Hexagon Press (PO Box 1302, Parramatta NSW, Australia), 1985.

_____. *Paul's Idea of Community: The Early House Churches in Their Historical Setting*, Grand Rapids, Mich.: Eerdmans, 1980.

Benne, Robert. *Ordinary Saints*, Philadelphia, Pa.: Fortress Press, 1988.

Fenhagen, James. *Mutual Ministry: New Vitality for the Local Church*, New York: Harper & Row, 1986.

Rowthorn, Anne. *The Liberation of the Laity*, Wilton, Conn.: Morehouse Publishers, 1986.

Stephens, Paul. *Liberating the Laity*, Downers Grove, Ill.: InterVarsity Press, 1985.

Trueblood, Elton. *The Company of the Committed*, New York: Harper & Row, 1980.

Biblical Egalitarianism

Bilezikian, Gilbert. *Beyond Sex Roles: What the Bible Says About a Woman's Place in Church and Family*, Grand Rapids, Mich.: Baker Book House, 1985.

Bristow, John Temple. *What Paul Really Said About Women*, New York: Harper & Row, 1988.

Gundry, Patricia. *Heirs Together: Mutual Submission in Marriage*, Grand Rapids, Mich.: Zondervan, 1988.

_____. *Woman Be Free! The Clear Message of Scripture*, Grand Rapids, Mich.: Zondervan, 1988.

Mickelsen, Alvera. *Women, Authority, and the Bible,* Downers Grove, Ill.: InterVarsity Press, 1986.

Roberts, Mark. "Woman Shall be Saved: A Closer Look at 1 Timothy 2:15," *Theological Students Fellowship Bulletin,* Nov/Dec, 1981.

Schmidt, Alvin. *Veiled and Silenced,* Macon, Ga.: Mercer University Press, 1989.

Spencer, Aida Besancon. "Eve at Ephesus: Should Women Be Ordained as Pastors According to the First Letter to Timothy?" *Journal of the Evangelical Theological Society,* 17, Fall, 1974.

_____. *Beyond the Curse: Women Called to Ministry,* Nashville, Tenn.: Thomas Nelson Publishers, 1985.

Church Buildings and Home Churches

Banks, Robert and Julia. *The Church Comes Home: Regrouping the People of God for Community and Missions,* Urbana, Ill.: Albatross, 1986.

Barrett, Lois. *Building the House Church,* Scottdale, Pa.: Herald Press, 1986.

Birkey, Del. *The House Church,* Scottdale, Pa.: Herald Press, 1988.

Eller, Vernard. *The Outward Bound: Caravaning as the Style of the Church,* Grand Rapids, Mich.: Eerdmans, 1980.

Lee, Bernard and Michael Cowan. *Dangerous Memories: House Churches and Our American Story,* Kansas City, Mo.: Sheed & Ward, 1986.

Maney, Thomas. *Basic Communities: A Practical Guide for Renewing Neighborhood Churches,* New York: Winston Press, 1984.

Snyder, Howard. *The Problem of Wineskins: Church Structure in a Technological Age,* Downers Grove, Ill.: InterVarsity Press, 1975.

Spirituality of Everyday Life

Banks, Robert. *All the Business of Life: Bringing Theology Down to Earth,* Urbana, Ill.: Albatross Books, 1987.

Boyer, Ernest. *Finding God at Home: Family Life as Spiritual Discipline,* New York: Harper & Row, 1988.

Haughey, John. *Converting 9 to 5: A Spirituality of Daily Work,* Freedom, Calif.: Crossroad, 1989.

Leckey, Dolores. *A Practical Spirituality for Lay People,* Kansas City, Mo.: Sheed & Ward, 1987.

Palmer, Parker. *The Active Life: a Spirituality of Work, Creativity, and Caring,* New York: Harper & Row, 1990.

Lifestyle Evangelism and the Contrast Culture Church

Krass, Alfred. *Evangelizing Neopagan North America*, Scottdale, Pa.: Herald Press, 1982.

Kraus, C. Norman. *The Authentic Witness*, Eerdmans/Herald Press, 1979.

Kraybill, Donald. *The Upside-Down Kingdom*, Scottdale, Pa.: Herald Press, rev. ed. 1990.

Seeliger, Wes. *Western Theology*, Houston, Tex.: Pioneer Ventures, 1973.

Sine, Tom. *Taking Discipleship Seriously*, Valley Forge, Pa.: Judson Press, 1985.

Wallis, Jim. *The Call to Conversion: Recovering the Gospel for These Times*, New York: Harper & Row, 1981.

The Christian Struggle for Social Justice

Gallardo, José. *The Way of Biblical Justice*, Scottdale, Pa.: Herald Press, 1983.

Mott, Stephen. *Biblical Ethics and Social Change*, Miami Beach, Fla.: Oxford, 1982.

Snyder, Howard. *Liberating the Church: The Ecology of Church and Kingdom*, Downers Grove, Ill.: InterVarsity Press, 1983.

_____. *A Kingdom Manifesto: Calling the Church to Live Under God's Reign*, Downers Grove, Ill.: InterVarsity Press, 1985.

Sider, Ronald. *Rich Christians in an Age of Hunger*, Waco, Tex.: Word, 1989.

Wallis, Jim. *Agenda for Biblical People*, New York: Harper & Row, 1976.

Wolterstorff, Nicholas. *Until Justice & Peace Embrace*, Grand Rapids, Mich.: Eerdmans, 1983.

To correspond with the author, and for information about communities and home churches in your area, write to:

Christian Smith
Department of Sociology
Gordon College
Wenham, MA   01984

Author

CHRISTIAN SMITH was born in
Abington, Pennsylvania, and grew up
in the Philadelphia area. He now lives
in Salem, Massachussets, and is assistant professor of sociology at Gordon
College (Wenham, Mass.).

Smith received M.A. and Ph.D. de-
grees from Harvard University (soci-
ology). He studied theology at the
Harvard Divinity School and took courses in theology at
Gordon Conwell Theological Seminary (South Hamilton,
Mass.) and the Andover Newton Theological School
(Andover, Mass.). He earned his bachelor's degree at Gor-
don College in 1983 and also attended Wheaton College
(Ill.) for two years.

Smith has traveled to Africa on a missions trip and to
Central and South America, and to England to do
sociological research. He has written an account of the
history of the liberation theology movement in Latin
America. He is now researching the 1980s United States-
based movement to oppose the United States-sponsored
war in Central America.

For twelve years Smith has been a member of Salem
Community Church, a network of house churches which
form an intentional Christian community. He is married to
Emily Jean Smith and has a son, Zachary Michael.